The Forward Book
of Poetry 1994

First published in Great Britain by
Forward Publishing · 5 Great Pulteney Street · London WIR 3DF
in association with
Sinclair-Stevenson, an imprint of Reed Consumer Books Ltd
Michelin House · 81 Fulham Road · London SW3 6RB
Auckland · Melbourne · Singapore · Toronto

ISBN 1 85619 425 6 (paperback)

Printed by Burrups Ltd
St Ives plc · London
Luxembourg · Paris · Tokyo

A CIP catalogue reference for this book
is available at the British Library.

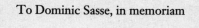

To Dominic Sasse, in memoriam

Preface

WHEN WE STARTED the Forward Poetry Prizes last year, we had
no idea that we would receive such support and enthusiasm from
poets, publishers and booksellers alike. The Forward Prizes are
now recognised as Britain's most important poetry competition
and this year's entries are nearly double those of last year's. Our
judges, Margaret Drabble, Cressida Connolly, Liz Lochhead,
Douglas Dunn and Blake Morrison, have had to absorb well over
a thousand poems before choosing the winners and selecting this
anthology.

This collection is designed to be a primer for those interested
in contemporary poetry. As such it shows not just the broad
range of styles and subject-matters that poets use but also, I
think, the healthy state of poetry in Britain and Ireland today.
Those who imagined that poetry has lost its way, please read on.

We have had help with the Prizes and this anthology from
many sources. In particular, I would like to thank Ellen
Hipschman at NASDAQ, an award winner under the Business
Sponsorship Incentive Scheme for its support of the Book Trust,
the administrator of the Prizes. The BSIS is a government
scheme administered by ABSA (Association of Business
Sponsorship of the Arts). I would also like to thank Richard
Lewis at Midland Bank who has helped to ensure that a copy
of the book goes out to every school and library in the country,
our co-sponsors Tim Waterstone and John Mitchinson at
Waterstone's, and Jeffery Tolman at Tolman Cunard.

Finally, I would like to thank: Christine Shaw, Sandra Vince
and Beverly Anderson at the Book Trust, Christopher Sinclair-
Stevenson, Neil Taylor, Angela Martin and Sarah Smyth at Reed
Books, Joanna Mackle at Faber and Faber and Emma Mahony,
Jo Douglas, Chantal MacRae, Robert Innes, Rebecca Cripps and
William Scott at Forward Publishing. Most of all I would like to
thank our judges for their hard work in selecting this anthology.

William Sieghart

Foreword

THIS IS THE second year of the Forward Poetry Prizes, and the second *Forward Book of Poetry*. This volume, like the last, contains a wide selection from the best of new contemporary poetry, and represents poets both familiar and unfamiliar, young and old. The judges read 130 collections, and about the same number of single poems published in magazines and periodicals. After much intense and amicable debate we arrived at this anthology, and decided on prize winners in three categories.

The judges this year were Cressida Connolly, Douglas Dunn, Liz Lochhead, Blake Morrison and myself: the prize winners were Carol Ann Duffy (£10,000 for best collection); Don Paterson (£5,000 for best first collection) and Vicki Feaver (£1,000 for a single poem). We were all very happy with our decisions, and pleased to have this opportunity of celebrating the work of these three poets.

The submissions were very varied, and came not only from well-established publishers with a tradition of publishing poetry, but also from small presses up and down the country. We were particularly pleased that some poets published by very small presses reached all our own personal shortlists, and are well represented in the anthology.

Reading through a year's output of poetry over a fairly short period is a fascinating exercise, and naturally gives rise to questions about how poets see themselves today – what preoccupies them, how they align themselves, and to what schools, if any, they belong. I think we all agreed that there was no dominant movement. The Scots, Irish and Welsh were powerfully represented, but their works did not fit neatly into any national groupings, any more than did the English – which ranged geographically from the back streets of Leicester and the Lincolnshire fens to Newcastle and Cornwall and Camden Town. The field was remarkably open, both in terms of style and content. We read sonnets, haiku, rhyming couplets, *terza rima*, lyrics, satires and elegies. We read poems of considerable verbal and metrical sophistication, and some of great simplicity. Occasionally the question would be asked: 'Is this poetry, or is it prose?' and a lively discussion would ensue. We hope the readers of this volume will enter the argument.

The subject-matter, as Stephen Spender said last year, was extremely varied. Anything goes. Some took on major public themes like Chernobyl, the Gulf War, the war in Yugoslavia, the break-up of Eastern Europe: it was impressive to note how many poets had recently been to Poland, the former Czechoslovakia, East Germany, Bulgaria. These poets are all British, but they belong to an international community and keep in touch with their colleagues. The poetry here represents a multi-cultural Britain, with a keen interest in the world beyond its own borders.

Other poets used domestic material, sometimes affectionately, sometimes ruefully, sometimes with disturbing implications, sometimes with pure rage. We had New Men writing about their babies; New Women writing about their lovers; sons mourning their fathers; daughters remembering their mothers. There were poems about apples and knitting and jam and refrigerators. There were poems about motorways and hospitals and gravedigging and old people in institutions. The contemporary world is well reflected here. We hope that readers will recognise it, and also see it more sharply as a result.

Poets may not be the conscience of the nation or the unacknowledged legislators of mankind. But, after this course of intensive reading, I myself felt that the best of them inhabit the world with quicker senses than most of us. In town or country, they see, smell and hear more. After a dulling daily diet of media platitudes, the poetry in this anthology puts us back in touch.

Margaret Drabble

Acknowledgements

Keith Ashton · DISABLED DAD GIVES DISABLED SON A SPORTING CHANCE · *Fair Moving* · Littlewood Arc

Donald Atkinson · IN SEARCH OF THE KRĒEN-AKRORĒ · *Graffiti for Hard Hearts* · Littlewood Arc

Iain Bamforth · WORDS OF ONE SYLLABLE · *Sons and Pioneers* · Carcanet

Colin Blundell · the citizens of the medieval republic · *invent the world* · Hub Editions 1993

Pat Boran · WAVING · *Familiar Things* · Dedalus

Jacqueline Brown · FAIRY TALE · *Thinking Egg* · Littlewood Arc

Andrea Capes · THE LAP DOG WITH THE LADY · *Home Fires* · Flambard

Vuyelwa Carlin · THE LEPERS OF LANGUEDOC · *Stand* · Summer 1992

Peter Cash · SWINESHEAD · *Fen Poems* · Staple First Edition

Fergus Chadwick · ENGLISH DISCOVERY · *A Shape in the Net* · Peterloo Poets

Gillian Clarke · ANOREXIC · *The King of Britain's Daughter* · Carcanet

John Clifford · LUCK · Phras Competition Magazine · June 1993

Gladys Mary Coles · HERON IN THE ALYN · *The Glass Island* · Duckworth

Tim Cumming · VIRTUAL REALITY · *Apocalypso* · Scratch

Tony Curtis · PORTRAIT OF THE PAINTER HANS THEO RICHTER AND HIS WIFE GISELA IN DRESDEN 1933 · Poetry Review

Fred D'Aguiar · AT THE GRAVE OF THE UNKNOWN AFRICAN · *British Subjects* · Bloodaxe

Sylvia Dann · BACK TO NATURE · *Back to Nature* · Jackson's Arm

Jonathan Davidson · NOW WE ARE MARRIED · *Moving the Stereo* · Jackson's Arm

Kirkpatrick Dobie · SUMMERFIELD · *Selected Poems* · Peterloo Poets

Ian Dudley · ABRACADABRA · *The Apple* · Envoi Poets Publications

Carol Ann Duffy · FRAUD · VALENTINE · THE CLICHÉ KID · *Mean Time* · Anvil

Paul Durcan · FATHER'S DAY, 21 JUNE 1992 · *A Snail in My Prime* ·
Harvill HarperCollins

Steve Ellis · RUBBISH · *West Pathway* · Bloodaxe

Vicki Feaver · JUDITH · *Independent on Sunday* · November 1992

Duncan Forbes · RECENSION DAY · *The Observer* · September 1992

Matthew Francis · OUTSIDE MY WINDOW · Harvest 1992

John Gohorry · A LETTER TO LADY PECUNIA · *Talk Into the Late Evening* ·
Peterloo Poets

Desmond Graham · MRS. THATCHER'S ENGLAND · *The Lie of Horizons* ·
Seren

Paul Groves · THE DIVINE CONTENDER · *Poetry Digest 61* · February 1993

David H.W. Grubb · TWO WEEKS AFTER MY FATHER'S DEATH WE PICK
THE PEARS · *The Rain Children* · Stride

John Gurney · AT THE PALMIST'S · Harvest 1992

Sophie Hannah · WRONG AGAIN · *The Frogmore Papers* · May 1993

Mike Harding · DADDY EDGAR'S POOLS · *Daddy Edgar's Pools* ·
Peterloo Poets

David Harsent · ELIMINATION DANCING · *News from the Front* ·
Oxford University Press

David Hartnett · THE FLEECE · *Dark Ages* · Secker & Warburg

Paul Henry · LEAVING TOWN · *Poetry Wales: Vol. 28, No. 2* ·
October 1992

Selima Hill · THE DEVASTATION OF EASTER ISLAND · *A Little Book of Meat* ·
Bloodaxe

Geoffrey Holloway · A SHEAF OF FLOWERS · 1992 Staple Open Poetry
Competition

Robert Hull · AXE · *Encouraging Shakespeare* · Peterloo Poets

Chris Hurford · RAY · *Heroes* · Polygon

Kathleen Jamie · THE PANCHEN LAMA RIDES FROM LHASA TO KUMBUM ·
The Autonomous Region · Bloodaxe

Lucien Jenkins · THE ENCLOSURE ACTS · *Laying Out The Body* · Seren

Mike Jenkins · *from* GRAFFITI NARRATIVES · Planet 96 (Dec.-Jan. 1992-93)

Sylvia Kantaris · ANIMALS · *Lad's Love* · Bloodaxe

David Kelly · RAW MEAT · *Poetry Digest* · February 1993

James Kirkup · HOMAGE TO RIMBAUD · *Words for Contemplation* · Cloud

Helen Kitson · ANOTHER NIGHT IN THE VICE SQUAD · *Seeing's Believing* · Scratch

Stephen Knight · THE BODY-PARTS LAUNDERETTE · *Flowering Limbs* · Bloodaxe

Aileen La Tourette · GIFT HORSES · *Poetry Review* · October 1992

Gwyneth Lewis · PENTECOST · *Poetry Review* · October 1992

Herbert Lomas · EGG ON A MANTELPIECE · *Trouble* · Sinclair-Stevenson

Roddy Lumsden · TWENTY HAIKU FOR MY DENTIST · *Poetry Introduction 8* · Faber and Faber

Glyn Maxwell · STARGAZING · *Poetry Review* · July 1993

Roger McGough · SQUARING UP · *Defying Gravity* · Viking

Jamie McKendrick · HOME THOUGHTS · *The Kiosk on the Brink* · Oxford University Press

Christine McNeill · SECOND LANGUAGE · *Kissing the Night* · Bloodaxe

Angela McSeveney · KIRSTY · *Coming Out With It* · Polygon

Christopher Middleton · LAMPOON · *The Balcony Tree* · Carcanet

Stuart Milson · BILLY AND THE PIGS · *Clonmel Writers' Week Open Poetry Competition Anthology*

Martin Mooney · GLASS · *Grub* · The Blackstaff Press

Paul Muldoon · *from* SHINING BROW · *Shining Brow* · Faber and Faber

Felicity Napier · JASMINE · *Acumen* · October 1992

Dennis O'Driscoll · MISUNDERSTANDING AND MUZAK · *Long Story Short* · Anvil

Don Paterson · THE FERRYMAN'S ARMS · SEED · NIL NIL · *Nil Nil* · Faber and Faber

Stuart Paterson · SECOND SKIN · *Chapman 71* · January 1993

Christopher Pilling · TIME FOR CHANGE · *Foreign Bodies* · Flambard

Stephen Plaice · LAST CAFÉ IN THE WEST · *Over the Rollers* · Yorick Books

Richard Price · HINGES · *Sense and a Minor Fever* · Vennel Press

Peter Redgrove · LAMPS AND FIRE · *The Laborators* · Taxus

Mark Robinson · DOMESTIC BLISS · *The Domesticity Remix* · Scratch

Stephen Romer · CAUTIONARY TALE · *Plato's Ladder* · Oxford
University Press

Carol Rumens · ET INCARNATUS EST · *Poetry Review* · July 1993

Carole Satyamurti · PASSED ON · *Independent on Sunday* · January 1993

William Scammell · TRIADS · *Five Easy Pieces* · Sinclair-Stevenson

Jo Shapcott · VEGETABLE LOVE · *Phrase Book* · Oxford University Press

Penelope Shuttle · THE READER · *Taxing the Rain* · Oxford
University Press

Stephen Smith · THE EXECUTION SHED · *The Fabulous Relatives* ·
Bloodaxe

Peter Street · STILLBORN · *Out of the Fire* · Spike Books

Matthew Sweeney · AFTER CLOSING TIME · *Cacti* · Secker & Warburg

R.S. Thomas · PLAS-YN-RHIW · *Mass for Hard Times* · Bloodaxe

Martin Turner · TRESPASSES · *Trespasses* · Faber and Faber

Steven Waling · FROM THE COUNTRY OF LOST HATS · *What the Snow
Believes* · Scratch

John Powell Ward · SPELLING · *A Certain Marvellous Thing* · Seren Books

Susan Wicks · HA HA BONK · *Singing Underwater* · Faber and Faber

Clive Wilmer · AMORES · *Of Earthly Paradise* · Carcanet

Chris Woods · BLOOD PRESSURE · *Recovery* · Enitharmon

Tamar Yoseloff · IN THE CHELSEA PHYSIC GARDEN · *Poetry Matters*
No. 10

Benjamin Zephaniah · MAN TO MAN · *City Psalms* · Bloodaxe

Contents

The Winning Poems

Carol Ann Duffy

FRAUD

Firstly, I changed my name
to that of a youth I knew for sure had bought it in 1940,
    Rotterdam.
Private M.
I was my own poem,
pseudonym,
rule of thumb.
What was my aim?
To change from a bum
to a billionaire. I spoke the English. Mine was a scam
involving pensions, papers, politicians in-and-out of their
    pram.
And I was to blame.

For what? There's a gnome
in Zürich knows more than people assume.
There's a military man, Jerusalem
way, keeping schtum.
Then there's Him –
for whom
I paid for a butch and femme
to make him come.
And all of the crème
de la crème
considered me scum.

Poverty's dumb.
Take it from me, Sonny Jim,
learn to lie in the mother-tongue of the motherfucker you
    want to charm.
They're all the same,
turning their wide blind eyes to crime.
And who gives a damn

when the keys to a second home
are pressed in his palm,
or polaroids of a Night of Shame
with a Boy on the Game
are passed his way at the A.G.M.?

So read my lips. Mo-ney. Pow-er. Fame.
And had I been asked, in my time,
in my puce and prosperous prime,
if I recalled the crumbling slum
of my Daddy's home,
if I was a shit, a sham,
if I'd done immeasurable harm,
I could have replied with a dream:
the water that night was calm
and with my enormous mouth, in bubbles and blood
      and phlegm,
I gargled my name.

VALENTINE

Not a red rose or a satin heart.

I give you an onion.
It is a moon wrapped in brown paper.
It promises light
like the careful undressing of love.

Here.
It will blind you with tears
like a lover.
It will make your reflection
a wobbling photo of grief.

I am trying to be truthful.

Not a cute card or a kissogram.

I give you an onion.
Its fierce kiss will stay on your lips,
possessive and faithful
as we are,
for as long as we are.

Take it.
Its platinum loops shrink to a wedding-ring,
if you like.
Lethal.
Its scent will cling to your fingers,
cling to your knife.

THE CLICHÉ KID

I need help, Doc, and bad; I can't forget
the rustle of my father's ballgown as he bent
to say goodnight to me, his kiss, his French scent...

Give me a shot of something. Or the sound of Ma
and her pals up late, boozing, dealing the cards.
Big Bertha pissing out from the porch under the stars...

It gets worse. Chalkdust. The old schoolroom empty.
This kid so unpopular even my imaginary friend left me
for another child. I'm screwed up, Doc, jumpy...

Distraught in autumn, kneeling under the chestnut trees,
seeing childhood in the conkers through my tears.
Bonkers. And me so butch in my boots down the macho
     bars...

Give me a break. Don't let me pine for that first love,
that faint down on the cheeks, that easy laugh
in my ears, in my lonesome heart, the day that I had to
     leave...

Sweet Jesus, Doc, I worry I'll miss when a long time dead
the smell the smell the smell of the baby's head,
the fresh-baked grass, dammit, the new-mown bread...

Don Paterson

THE FERRYMAN'S ARMS

About to sit down with my half-pint of Guinness
I was magnetized by a remote phosphorescence
and drawn, like a moth, to the darkened back room
where a pool-table hummed to itself in the corner.
With ten minutes to kill and the whole place deserted
I took myself on for the hell of it. Slotting
a coin in the tongue, I looked round for a cue –
while I stood with my back turned, the balls were
    deposited
with an abrupt intestinal rumble; a striplight
batted awake in its dusty green cowl.
When I set down the cue-ball inside the parched D
it clacked on the slate; the nap was so threadbare
I could screw back the globe, given somewhere to stand –
as physics itself becomes something negotiable
a rash of small miracles covers the shortfall:
I went on to make an immaculate clearance.
A low punch with a wee dab of side, and the black
did the vanishing trick while the white stopped
before gently rolling back as if nothing had happened,
shouldering its way through the unpotted colours.

The boat chugged up to the little stone jetty
without breaking the skin of the water, stretching,
as black as my stout, from somewhere unspeakable
to here, where the foaming lip mussitates endlessly,
trying, with a nutter's persistence, to read
and re-read the shoreline. I got aboard early,
remembering the ferry would leave on the hour
even for only my losing opponent;
but I left him there, stuck in his tent of light, sullenly
knocking the balls in, for practice, for next time.

SEED

Parenthood is no more than murder
by degrees, the classic martyr-
dom. All the old myths are true: I pushed him under,
scything his bollocks off, stealing his thunder.

Leaking cock or bodged withdrawal,
ruptured condom; month-long vigil –
it is I who just escape with my life.
My child is hunting me down like a thief.

NIL NIL

Just as any truly accurate representation of a particular
geography can only exist on a scale of 1:1 (imagine the
vast, rustling map of Burgundy, say, settling over it
like a freshly-starched sheet!) so it is with all our abandoned histories, those ignoble lines of succession that
end in neither triumph nor disaster, but merely plunge
on into deeper and deeper obscurity; only in the infinite ghost-libraries of the imagination – their only
possible analogue – can their ends be pursued, the dull
and terrible facts finally authenticated.
                        Francois Aussemain, Pensées

From the top, then, the zenith, the silent footage:
McGrandle, majestic in ankle-length shorts,
his golden hair shorn to an open book, sprinting
the length of the park for the long hoick forward,
his balletic toe-poke nearly bursting the roof
of the net; a shaky pan to the Erskine St End
where a plague of grey bonnets falls out of the clouds.
But ours is a game of two halves, and this game
the semi they went on to lose; from here
it's all down, from the First to the foot of the Second,
McGrandle, Visocchi and Spankie detaching
like bubbles to speed the descent into pitch-sharing,
pay-cuts, pawned silver, the Highland Division,
the absolute sitters ballooned over open goals,
the dismal nutmegs, the scores so obscene
no respectable journal will print them; though one day
Farquhar's spectacular bicycle-kick
will earn him a name-check in Monday's obituaries.
Besides the one setback – the spell of giant-killing
in the Cup (Lochee Violet, then Aberdeen Bon Accord,
the deadlock with Lochee Harp finally broken

by Farquhar's own-goal in the replay)
nothing inhibits the fifty-year slide
into Sunday League, big tartan flasks,
open hatchbacks parked squint behind goal-nets,
the half-time satsuma, the dog on the pitch,
then the Boy's Club, sponsored by Skelly Assurance,
then Skelly Dry Cleaners, then nobody;
stud-harrowed pitches with one-in-five inclines,
grim fathers and perverts with Old English Sheepdogs
lining the touch, moaning softly.
Now the unrefereed thirty-a-sides,
terrified fat boys with callipers minding
four jackets on infinite, notional fields;
ten years of dwindling, half-hearted kickabouts
leaves two little boys – Alastair Watt,
who answers to 'Forty', and wee Horace Madden,
so smelly the air seems to quiver above him –
playing desperate two-touch with a bald tennis ball
in the hour before lighting-up time.
Alastair cheats, and goes off with the ball
leaving wee Horace to hack up a stone
and dribble it home in the rain;
past the stopped swings, the dead shanty-town
of allotments, the black shell of Skelly Dry Cleaners
and into his cul-de-sac, where, accidentally,
he neatly back-heels it straight into the gutter
then tries to swank off like he meant it.

Unknown to him, it is all that remains
of a lone fighter-pilot, who, returning at dawn
to find Leuchars was not where he'd left it,
took time out to watch the Sidlaws unsheathed
from their great black tarpaulin, the haar burn off Tayport
and Venus melt into Carnoustie, igniting
the shoreline; no wind, not a cloud in the sky
and no one around to admire the discretion
of his unscheduled exit: the engine plopped out

and would not re-engage, sending him silently
twirling away like an ash-key,
his attempt to bail out only partly successful,
yesterday having been April the 1st –
the ripcord unleashing a flurry of socks
like a sackful of doves rendered up to the heavens
in private irenicon. He caught up with the plane
on the ground, just at the instant the tank blew
and made nothing of him, save for his fillings,
his tackets, his lucky half-crown and his gallstone,
now anchored between the steel bars of a stank
that looks to be biting the bullet on this one.

In short, this is where you get off, reader;
I'll continue alone, on foot, in the failing light
following the trail as it steadily fades
into road-repairs, birdsong, the weather, nirvana,
the plot thinning down to a point so refined
not even the angels could dance on it. Goodbye.

Vicki Feaver

JUDITH

Wondering how a good woman can murder
I enter the tent of Holofernes,
holding in one hand his long oiled hair
and in the other, raised above
his sleeping, wine-flushed face,
his falchion with its unsheathed
curved blade. And I feel a rush
of tenderness, a longing
to put down my weapon, to lie
sheltered and safe in a warrior's
fumey sweat, under the emerald stars
of his purple and gold canopy,
to melt like a sweet on his tongue
to nothing. And I remember the glare
of the barley field; my husband
pushing away the sponge I pressed
to his burning head; the stubble
puncturing my feet as I ran,
flinging myself on a body
that was already cooling
and stiffening; and the nights
when I lay on the roof – my emptiness
like the emptiness of a temple
with the doors kicked in; and the mornings
when I rolled in the ash of the fire
just to be touched and dirtied
by something. And I bring my blade
down on his neck – and it's easy
like slicing through fish.
And I bring it down again,
cleaving the bone.

Other Poems

Keith Ashton

Disabled Dad Gives Disabled Son a Sporting Chance

Remember the foot-tapping rides you gave?
Me a tonweight on your toe-ends? Rare kind
of bucking bronco, you took pains to save

me from falling; and never seemed to mind
scant rough and tumble with your son and heir.
Horseplay, to all intents, was unconfined.

Then, stacked against booth-boxing at the Fair
and bouts for the Navy, your sudden gift
of gloves became eight ounces more to share.

Cross-legged, I sat, a flyweight launching swift
left hooks, half unaware of knocks you took
from arms encouragement helped barely lift.

You saw good in the fight put up. I shook
medals raided from your bottom drawer, hit
upon cutting them to ribbons. Some nook

down some backyard perhaps still perfect fit
for silver and bronze and trimmings to rot,
just the case survives, a party-piece, split.

Misfortune and war broke your heart, each shot
at goal, come peacetime, costing dear. Carried
from the pitch finally, left only what

the sports Echo said, Ashton had harried
his ultimate 'keeper – or so it seemed –
life in the balance and newly married.

Yet, many years on you blazed a trail, teamed
for five minutes with younger men one man
short. Opposition, out to stop subs, steamed

in with a vengeance. You lengthened stride, ran
rings round sweepers – nearly. No cause to doubt
who left them standing, back when games began!

For two pins, still, I'd kick a ball about
with you as – gloveless now – we love to spar.
Given half a chance, willingly, I'd flout

the law of averages; smooth the scar
of disability; carry the fight.
Trainer-managed, your boy would be a star.

As it is, no high point betters the night
we sped down to earth, a clean pair of heels
from The Jolly Sailor, chair on two wheels,
you setting pace in a world out of sight.

Donald Atkinson

IN SEARCH OF THE KRĒEN-AKRORĒ
an anthropological exploration

In this vile terrain
Progress is slow.
It takes each mile of pain
All day to go.

Through the dank rain-
Forest I cleave my track.
Behind me the leaves close
Hiding the way back.

At night trees full of eyes
Gird me with stares.
I cannot tell which of the birds' cries
Are really theirs.

By day these timid spies
Take fright and melt away.
Quite where your tribal village lies
Maps do not say.

I go by the small signs
A single snapped stalk;
The glyph of faint lines
Left on a tree's bark.

Only today I crept
Well-meaning and too late
Into your empty camp. You slept
And ate

Here last night, then left.
Sensing me near,
Suspecting rape, disease or theft,
You fled in fear.

Therefore with hesitance
Soliciting trust
I hang my tin presents
In your deserted huts.

Will my useful gifts
Tease from your raised fist
An open hand, or release a swift
Spear's thrust?

Simian voices wake
Those azure birds to sing.
You're there. You've come to take
All that I bring.

Alert child, cradled in serpents.
Lips licked by a sting.
How will your Argus eyes interpret
Their own opening?

Friendless,
Apart,
Is your first essay in dependence
About to start?

Return
Strange envoy of the Kreen-Akrore
And unlearn. For the story
Of the pain is endless.

Do not look round.
No footsteps swallow
The trail you lay.
Your heartland's safe from being found.
No-one will follow.

Iain Bamforth

WORDS OF ONE SYLLABLE

Who knows why they leave, but they do.
The wind flaps, and gives no sign
though the risk breathes a hint of wolf.
They boast, they limp out on a curse
though they can't tell which. Sheep look up
coal-faced, at the edge of the deep.

They yawn, they nod, they look and loom,
 and love, it goes to a dark shed.
This is the word, and this is the life
spat on, got through, worn out, gone from.
Old hats are damp where heads are:
deep in the ground, dense in the air.

Dark folds of days would mean as much.
Small fish get worked to the bone.
And down the mines, the air is sour;
grown cold, it creeps in the door
to tea and scones. They feed on that,
sit side by side, and talk true grit.

Who knows, the days could mean no worse.
The harm is done and sons go out
though they walk on salt and dig for less.
Faces at the door are all at sea
when one says, dear, it'll be fine but.
Now they leave not a word says not.

Colin Blundell

the citizens of the medieval republic

were certainly under the limitation
of only being asked to die
for the things with which
they had always lived:
the houses they inhabited;
the shrines they venerated;
the rulers and representatives they knew

they had not the larger vision
calling them to die for
the latest rumours about remote colonies
as reported in anonymous newspapers

and if we infer from our own experience
that war paralyses civilisation
we must at least admit
that these warring towns turned out
a number of paralytics
who go by the names of Dante
and Michelangelo   Ariosto and Titian
Leonardo and Columbus   not to mention
Catherine of Sienna and Francis of Assisi

about three-quarters of the greatest people
who ever lived came out of
these little towns
and were often engaged
in these little wars

it remains to be seen
what will ultimately come out of
our large towns;
but there has been no sign

of anything of this sort
since they became large

I have sometimes been haunted
by a fancy of my youth
that these things will not come
till there is a city wall
round Clapham
and the tocsin is rung at night
to arm the citizens of Wimbledon

After G.K. Chesterton: St Francis of Assisi

Pat Boran

WAVING

As a child I waved to people I didn't know.
I waved from passing cars, school buses,
second-floor windows, or from the street
to secretaries trapped in offices above.
When policemen motioned my father on
past the scene of the crime or an army checkpoint,
I waved back from the back seat. I loved to wave.
I saw the world disappear into a funnel
of perspective, like the reflection in a bath
sucked into a single point when the water
drains. I waved in greeting at things that vanished
into points. I waved to say, 'I see you: can you see me?'

I loved 'the notion of an ocean' that could wave,
of a sea that rose up to see the onlooker
standing on the beach. And though the sea
came towards the beach, it was a different sea
when it arrived; the onlooker too had changed.
They disappeared, both of them, into points in time.
So that was why they waved to one another.
On the beach I waved until my arms hurt.

My mother waved her hair sometimes. This,
I know, seems to be something else. But,
when she came up the street, bright and radiant,
her white hair like a jewel-cap on her head,
it was a signal I could not fail to answer.
I waved and she approached me, smiling shyly.

Sometimes someone walking beside her
might wave back, wondering where they knew me from.
Hands itched in pockets, muscles twitched
when I waved. 'There's someone who sees me!'

But in general people took no risk with strangers.
And when they saw who I was – or wasn't –
they felt relief, saved from terrible disgrace.

Now it turns out that light itself's a wave
(as well as a point, or points), so though the waving's
done, it's really only just beginning. Whole humans –
arms, legs, backs, bellies – are waving away,
flickering on and off, in and out of time
and space, pushing through streets with heads down,
smiling up at office windows, lying in gutters
with their kneecaps broken and their hopes dashed,
driving, loving, hiding, growing old, and always
waving, waving as if to say: 'Can you see me?
I can see you – still... still... still...'

Jacqueline Brown

FAIRY TALE

There are trees. She slinks
among them with an empty belly.
There is a house that is bursting
with kids. The kids' mother
has gone off shopping. She is a bad mother,
leaving her kids thus. She would
not miss a kid. One soft milky
kid less would mean nothing to her.

A story mothers read to children
before sleeping, starting *Once*
upon a time, starting like memory
at no-date, no-place, no-time.

There is a door. She knocks on the door
raprap, pleading for, wanting in.
But the kids are good kids.
The kids are wise in the ways of tales.
They demand to see her fingers.
Dipped in flour, her fingers are white
as a mother's, white as a nanny's.

You can imagine it from their point of view –
the sneck lifted, the flurry, the panicky cries,
their sharp hooves' scatter…
a memory they'll consign to blankness,
to the hot dark they can only grope after.

Look how her belly has swollen now.
Look at the silly content smile as she sleeps.
Imagine her point of view when she wakens
in the black of the well-shaft, the pinpoint sky
that could be a million miles away
and her belly packed to bursting with stones.

Andrea Capes

THE LAP DOG WITH THE LADY

I should have bitten his fingers that first time,
serve him right, and none of this would have happened.
But I'm trained from youth to behave myself.
So when he flirted with me, then with her,
beckoned then dismissed me all in play,
all I could do was growl, obey the tug
Anna Sergeyevna gave my leash and hear
her say – He doesn't bite – invite him
to admire my thick white Pomeranian fur.
If only my life were different – hunts,
farmyards, the world of real smells, fighting –
anything but this boredom she calls ennui.
Days of lying under café tables or at heel
along the Esplanade. An afterthought,
a lapdog bought so a wife alone in Yalta
for the summer would appear less alone.

Flirtation and a quick seduction,
but they couldn't enjoy even that –
people might learn a thing or two from us –
his boredom with her guilt and tears, his mis-
givings, I had to sit through all of this.
Imagine my surprise one winter morning
when I came down the steps and sniffed then
saw him by the long grey fence outside our house.
What else could he want, a Muscovite,
in a place as godforsaken as this town of S— ?
I ignored him, once was enough for me.
He didn't call my name, I'm glad to say.
I see her grow old with love fuelled by their
secrecy, frustration, my master's suspicion.
The hopelessness is what they seem to want.

That first summer I recall we were watched
by a man who sat at the next table, alone,
couldn't take his eyes off the two of them.
Another admirer was what I thought and I'd
have to go through with my show of guarding her,
growl, raise my hackles, all over again.
But he just looked at them and at me too,
and I'm only a dog, as if he saw the whole story
unravel right there in front of him.
And he should watch that little cough of his,
a doctor who smells of illness, daydreams
his time away at restaurant tables.
What a way to spend one's life, he seemed to say,
but not unkindly. And what encounters life offers.

Vuyelwa Carlin

The Lepers of Languedoc

We blued, livid, and our children
went to God, all bruisy – He took them so quickly! –
It was our despair to blame, our anger
at the scant grain, the bread all cobbled

of stalks and skin. – And the rich were greedy,
nugget-hearts, lacked
love of Heaven. – I know this, know it:
– yet we herded them, the blotched creatures,

crying, all raggle-taggle
with their handbells, – lit huge fires
for the burning of them, tainted things
so it is told. – No running away, they were clumpy,

blind, lumpfeet. – All is bleak: God seems cruel –
our children dead, clutching
their herbs, and this black smoke: – these wretches,
the poorest, cracking, bursting of our sickness.

In Languedoc during the Black Death epidemic of 1321, all the lepers
were burnt, on suspicion of poisoning the wells.

Peter Cash

SWINESHEAD

I'll tell thee, Hubert, half my power this night,
Passing these flats, are taken by the tide;
These Lincoln Washes have devoured them.
    King John Act V Scene VI

We come too fast for the A52:
    towards Bicker Fen, an inconguous spire
    grows heavenwards into grandeur
and hints at aspirations that require

an unironic chronicler.
    Spectacular above beet-fields, it speaks
    of an age before an austere -ism
took root among these crops that weeks

of April rain have water-logged;
    it points to an epoch when not even skies
    were their limits. As we coast past,
those ancient pieties

seem to have dissolved into the soil,
    sunk into pre-history.
    Cabbage-cutters, wearing leather-jerkins,
take out muddy flasks of tea

and talk in monosyllables.
    What quietens us both
    is that – although they nearly drown –
    they never think to wave
    at interested drivers who slow down.
Drizzle drags its dish-cloth

across their closed expressions,

their cadaverous faces.
    Each head-scarfed woman ekes
out her frugal existence, places

little value on the legacy
    of which she is an in-bred part.
    Beyond her, in the distance,
Market Place beats like a by-passed heart....

Diocese of derelict farm-buildings:
    for now, St Mary's spire soars
    over its undismantled past
    without attenuation.
Dark sheds and old shop-fronts resist
both my exegeses and yours.

Fergus Chadwick

ENGLISH DISCOVERY

I study the map, its sweet smell
and sour shock, the boss
of its pink and scarlet shield, polished
with my cuff under moonlight
to a smiling wax, gravely enceinte:
the disconnected globe, from blossom
wet in the grass, showing its green
continents, its gold-red walls of fire.

It is as I say the pallor of orchards,
the tissue fruit are wrapped in:
but this sweet smell, tempting my teeth
to open the round volume, and find
a place in its glistening snows,
whose flavour carves out cliffs
sharp as alchy cider juice,
wins back my boyhood, apple years.

All the years are apple years, eaten
by moonlight: but this chomp
in a windfall, its sweet smell
and sour shock, its cordillera of pulp,
reads out a seashore, a silver plane
flying over a coast, a car-ride home,
a gate, a tidal wave of August
trees, curved over grass intensely green.

And this hand – closing on an apple,
pulling down tight-fisted reds
each with a bursting golden rocket
in a crimson sky, climbing still
through leaves up sinewy boles –
must contemplate itself a boy's:

a prisoner in the central cage
whose white pips are eaten round.

Gillian Clarke

ANOREXIC

My father's sister,
the one who died
before there was a word for it,
was fussy with her food.
'Eat up,' they'd say to me,
ladling a bowl with warning.

What I remember's
how she'd send me to the dairy,
taught me to take cream,
the standing gold.
Where the jug dipped
I saw its blue-milk skin
before the surface healed.

Breath held, tongue between teeth,
I carried in the cream,
brimmed, level,
parallel, I knew,
with that other, hidden horizon
of the earth's deep
ungleaming water-table.

And she, more often than not half-dressed,
stockings, a slip, a Chinese kimono,
would warm the cream, pour it
with crumbled melting cheese
over a delicate white cauliflower,
or field mushrooms
steaming in porcelain,

then watch us eat, relishing,
smoking her umpteenth cigarette,

glamorous, perfumed, starved,
and going to die.

John Clifford

LUCK

On the building site at midday,
We sat round a packing case
And played cards while the tea brewed,
Paddy and Tiny White and Neverfuck and me.
We laid down the cards, one by one,
Each card a day's life,
And tight in our hands we held the rest of our days.

Red days and black days were scattered on the box,
Put down softly or carelessly or with a bang;
And Paddy is crushed between a truck and a wall,
And Tiny White is unemployed and bitter,
And Neverfuck a sour wizened old husk,
And I have smooth hands and a soft job,
For so the cards were dealt and so they fell.

Perhaps with luck it could have been quite different;
Paddy happily drunk in a pub in Sligo,
Tiny in a suit, taking home real money,
Neverfuck happy in some peculiar way,
And for myself no need to feel a traitor.
That is how I would have dealt the cards
If I had known, and if it had been my deal.

But *these* are the cards, smeared with thumb marks,
Torn corners, hard used every day,
Like Paddy, Tiny, Neverfuck and me.
And this is the game, and this the building site,
And these the dirty times we live in;
And if we are going to change our luck and win –
This is where we must start.

Gladys Mary Coles

HERON IN THE ALYN

I follow the river, heron-seeking
where weed and nettle reign,
caught in my sorrows
and my imagined sorrows.
Flies flick and rise, torment
slow cattle. Willows trail the water
and floating celandine; maybe also Ophelia
singing *'O, you must wear your rue
with a difference.'*

Seeking the heron
I make unexpected finds –
the sludge of a water-rat's lair,
sheep's wool a ragged veil on wire,
a tree-wound colonised by fungus –
and suddenly I see the secret bird!

Hidden in a tanglebend,
grey visitant in fish-vigil,
alert in the afternoon heat.
Such startled lift-off
of great wings, crashing
through boughs, attaining sky.

I watch the slow pulse
of its flight, the laboured ease,
diminishing into distance
with its weight of unseen freight –
my sorrows, my imagined sorrows.

Tim Cumming

VIRTUAL REALITY

She calls from the bathroom,
"Come and squeeze a spot on my back
and talk dirty to me."
I'm watching The Rough Guide to High Living
on the hotel television
thinking of our absent friends
with their long line of dramatic entrances.
I tell her I would love to talk dirty, but I can't
remember her name.
We've really worked at it this time.
She comes in and pulls off the duvet,
spilling a carton of orange juice and vodka.
"I like it like that," I say, "Do it again."
 Our language isn't so dirty, but it's our language.
The bed is strewn with our holiday memorabilia;
the handwritten note that said,
The dancing bear could be yours for a fortnight.
Later I pull on a wolf-mask
and lean over the champagne to kiss her cheek.
My fingers hunt for a light switch.
Then I remember we do this with the lights on.

Tony Curtis

PORTRAIT OF THE PAINTER HANS THEO RICHTER
AND HIS WIFE GISELA IN DRESDEN 1933

This is the perfect moment of love
Her arm around his neck
Holds a rose.

Her wisps of yellow hair
The light turns gold.
Her face is the moon to his earth.

Otto's studio wall glows
With the warm wheat glow
Of the loving couple.

This is after the dark etchings,
The blown faces. This is after Bapaume –
The sickly greens, the fallen browns.

She is a tree, her neck a swan's curved to him.
His hands enclose her left hand
Like folded wings.

This is before the fire-storm,
Before the black wind,
The city turned to broken teeth.

It is she who holds the rose to him,
Theo's eyes which lower in contentment
To the surgeon's smock he has for painting.

This is the perfect moment,
The painted moment
She will not survive.

This is before the hair that flames,
The face that chars. This is before
Her long arms blacken like winter boughs.

This is the harvest of their love,
It is summer in the soul,
The moment they have made together.

From Otto's window the sounds of the day –
The baker's boy calling, a neighbour's wireless
playing marches and then a speech.

Fred D'Aguiar

At the Grave of the Unknown African

1

Two round, cocoa faces, carved on whitewashed headstone
protect your grave against hellfire and brimstone.

Those cherubs with puffed cheeks, as if chewing gum,
signal how you got here and where you came from.

More than two and a half centuries after your death,
the barefaced fact that you're unnamed feels like defeat.

I got here via White Ladies Road and Black Boy's Hill,
clues lost in these lopsided stones that Henbury's vandal

helps to the ground and Henbury's conservationist
tries to rectify, cleaning the vandal's pissy love-nest.

African slave without a name, I'd call this home
by now. Would you? Your unknown soldier's tomb

stands for shipload after shipload that docked,
unloaded, watered, scrubbed, exercised and restocked

thousands more souls for sale in Bristol's port;
cab drivers speak of it all with yesterday's hurt.

The good conservationist calls it her three hundred year
war;
those raids, deals, deceit and capture (a sore still raw).

St Paul's, Toxteth, Brixton, Tiger Bay and Handsworth:
petrol bombs flower in the middle of roads, a sudden growth

at the feet of police lines longer than any cricket pitch.
African slave, your namelessness is the wick and petrol
     mix.

Each generation catches the one fever love can't appease;
nor Molotov cocktails, nor when they embrace in a peace

far from that three-named, two-bit vandal and conserva-
     tionist
binning beer cans, condoms and headstones in big puzzle-
     pieces.

2

Stop there black Englishman before you tell a bigger lie.
You mean me well by what you say but I can't stand idly by.

The vandal who keeps coming and does what he calls fucks
on the cool gravestones, also pillages and wrecks.

If he knew not so much my name but what happened to
     Africans,
he'd maybe put in an hour or two collecting his Heinekens;

like the good old conservationist, who's earned her column
inch, who you knock, who I love without knowing her name.

The dead can't write, nor can we sing (nor can most living).
Our ears (if you can call them ears) make no good listening.

Say what happened to me and countless like me, all anon.
Say it urgently. Mean times may bring back the water cannon.

I died young, but to age as a slave would have been worse.
What can you call me? Mohammed. Homer. Hannibal. Jesus.

Would it be too much to have them all? What are couples up to when one reclines on the stones and is ridden by the other?

Will our talk excite the vandal? He woz *ere, like you are now,*
armed with a knife, I could see trouble on his creased brow,

love-trouble, not for some girl but for this village.
I share his love and would have let him spoil my image,

if it wasn't for his blade in the shadow of the church wall
taking me back to my capture and long sail to Bristol,

then my sale on Black Boy's Hill and disease ending my days:
I sent a rumble up to his sole; he scooted, shocked and dazed.

Here the sentence is the wait and the weight is the sentence.
I've had enough of a parish where the congregation can't sing.

Take me where the hymns sound like a fountain-washed
      canary,
and the beer-swilling, condom wielding vandal of Henbury,

reclines on the stones and the conservationist mounts him,
and in my crumbly ears there's only the sound of them sinning.

Sylvia Dann

BACK TO NATURE

It's 2.00 am and after several cans
of Tennents we're getting a bit
philosophical Jim says he'll pack in
writing songs and go up the Amazon
in a canoe Mike says he fancies
lying around all day in the forest getting
pissed on jungle juice and Brendan says
that when they're all too smashed to go out
and kill a creature they'll send the
women off to gather berries they ask what
will you do I say I'll teach the women
to be assertive so they can tell you to
fuck off and pick your own berries.

Jonathan Davidson

Now We Are Married

You have polished the cut glass vase
and the two rose bowls. I am ironing
because if I have cooked I will not
wash-up, unless you have vacuumed,
which you will do only if the yard
has been swept within the last week.
When I either remove or rebuild
the ex-post-office bicycle
under the stairs you will consider
filing your correspondence. Today
I would grout tiles, but I have not
because I understood the bathroom
was within your jurisdiction,
in which case I would happily
take charge of the study, if we had
one. As we do not I had agreed
to see to the decorative glassware.
I do the decorative glassware.
Therefore, I ask, why have you polished
the two rose bowls and the cut glass vase?

Kirkpatrick Dobie

Summerfield

Tall poppies grow beside the stile,
some partly hidden by the hedge,
and some that brush the upper rail
are rooted at the very edge.

In June of every year they come
red-orange-tipped and irised-brown.
They sway towards you as you pass
and touch your hand as you step down.

Great gangling girls, they never learn
how much of men is purely brute,
so every year they come again
and some are trampled underfoot.

Ian Dudley

ABRACADABRA

The sun picks our conscience clean; a copper
light tempered in blood. The blue tiles and mud
walls of their houses stare across the valley,
closer to us than any memory of home.

Mosques, minarets, groves of pomegranate;
Jalalabad: the abracadabra
of language and place. We have no place here:
the barbarians live at the glittering

edge of the blade – the whetted billhook,
the burnished runnels of irrigation,
the crack of light at dawn and dusk calling

to obeisance. Dispossessed we repossess
their landscape overwritten in Cyrillic:
Kalashnikov, the curt stuttering script.

Paul Durcan

FATHER'S DAY, 21 JUNE 1992

Just as I was dashing to catch the Dublin-Cork train,
Dashing up and down the stairs, searching my pockets,
She told me that her sister in Cork wanted a loan of the
    axe;
It was late June and
The buddleia tree in the backyard
Had grown out of control.
The taxi was ticking over outside in the street,
All the neighbours noticing it.
"You mean that you want me to bring her down the axe?"
"Yes, if you wouldn't mind, that is –"
"A simple saw would do the job, surely to God
She could borrow a simple saw."
"She said that she'd like the axe."
"OK. There is a Blue Cabs taxi ticking over outside
And the whole world inspecting it,
I'll bring her down the axe."
The axe – all four-and-a-half feet of it –
Was leaning up against the wall behind the settee –
The fold-up settee that doubles as a bed.
She handed the axe to me just as it was,
As neat as a newborn babe,
All in the bare buff.
You'd think she'd have swaddled it up
In something – if not a blanket, an old newspaper,
But no, not even a token hanky
Tied in a bow round its head.
I decided not to argue the toss. I kissed her goodbye.

The whole long way down to Cork
I felt uneasy. Guilt feelings.
It's a killer, this guilt.
I always feel bad leaving her

But this time it was the worst.
I could see that she was glad
To see me go away for a while,
Glad at the prospect of being
Two weeks on her own,
Two weeks of having the bed to herself,
Two weeks of not having to be pestered
By my coarse advances,
Two weeks of not having to look up from her plate
And behold me eating spaghetti with a knife and fork.
Our daughters are all grown up and gone away.
Once when she was sitting pregnant on the settee
It snapped shut with herself inside it,
But not a bother on her. I nearly died.

As the train slowed down approaching Portarlington
I overheard myself say to the passenger sitting opposite
      me:
"I am feeling guilty because she does not love me
As much as she used to, can you explain that?"
The passenger's eyes were on the axe on the seat beside
      me.
"Her sister wants a loan of the axe…"
As the train threaded itself into Portarlington
I nodded to the passenger "Cúl an tSúdaire!"
The passenger stood up, lifted down a case from the rack,
Walked out of the coach, but did not get off the train.
For the remainder of the journey, we sat alone,
The axe and I,
All the green fields running away from us,
All our daughters grown up and gone away.

Steve Ellis

RUBBISH

I

I fed the refuse of my baby
to the fire, its awful red
starting to taste the edges,
a slow, cool savour;

and then it changed gear
like some brutish car,
surging and speeding
round the white lump.

I thought: purification.
Here's this shitty nappy,
lamb and carrot aftermath,
I touch it to the jewels.

And they just laugh into flame,
are stoked into beauty.
I thought of great plagues,
human flesh festering

and bright feeding fire
that turns pus to gold,
the body's rotten debris
into warm, clean ash.

The gift of incineration.
Then I thought, holocaust.
Then I saw there's no end
for this poem, but the fire.

II

Then I plucked it out.
I thought: I'll re-route it
from the horrors of history
via a little social comedy.

Viz: in my father's house
the nappy-sack is a stranger,
that delicate, perfumed bag
dainty of dustbinmen.

Here in the harsh North
even the black bin-liner
is rarely seen; parings,
meal slops, cut toenails,

the cat's sick, all straight in
splat on the naked metal,
that rusts nights in the yard
earning its grim keep.

Maw open to the heavens.
But even the municipal bin
is a modern brainwave,
which brings me back to fire.

Once, one and only disposer;
I sift back through centuries
watching your prowess,
all-comers' knight-devourer.

Two nappies have arrived now.
I think: it'll never eat that!
Licks lips, effortlessly.
Braggadocio digestion.

Duncan Forbes

Recension Day

Unburn the boat, rebuild the bridge,
Reconsecrate the sacrilege,
Unspill the milk, decry the tears,
Turn back the clock, relive the years
Replace the smoke inside the fire,
Unite fulfilment with desire,
Undo the done, gainsay the said,
Revitalise the buried dead,
Revoke the penalty and clause,
Reconstitute unwritten laws,
Repair the heart, untie the tongue,
Change faithless old to hopeful young,
Inure the body to disease
And help me to forget you please.

Matthew Francis

Outside my Window

In the shaped darkness where I used to be,
something is shouting. I'm awake. The voice
is a girl swearing in the not-quite place
you have to cross to get back home today.

It is a place that wants to be elsewhere.
You never think about it till one night
you leave the pub or party, and the street
is stretched out waiting for you. It is here,

empty and cold, your sleeping theatre,
rinsed with a lamplit silence which you share
with everyone who's stood out here before.
Some bastard starts to play a bass guitar.

Sounds like he's playing over the telephone,
a hollow, basement music that you feel
rather than hear. Ponderous. Comical.
You'll be all right in a minute. You'll just lean

on somebody's gatepost till you get your breath
back, while the houses stand not holding theirs.
You clench your jacket, ready. This is yours,
this stretch of midnight, to do something with.

It is a long receptacle of shouts.
Now you feel better, don't you? Now they know,
the upstairs dreamers, that you live here, too.
Your words run naked through their curtained nights.

And then you go home and you go to sleep.
The whole town sleeps together, except them,
that hoarse, white company you can't unscream.

They stand outside your house and wake you up,

you being me. Now it's years later. The face
is someone else's, but the same words still
wrench it apart. What are they after? Well,
they've done with me now and I want some peace.

I'm heading for the other side of what
I take to be a sort of game reserve
full of bird-noises and the whining of
that bug the milk-float settling on the street.

John Gohorry

A Letter to Lady Pecunia

Dear Lady,
        My name probably won't mean very much
to you, although I regularly keep in touch
with your champagne breakfasts and intimate suppers,
being an avid reader of the quality newspapers.

I have followed your fortunes and your affairs
devotedly – studied your portfolios of shares
and investment accounts with building societies
like a distant suitor calculating the niceties

of advantage for his remote beloved's prosperity.
I have wished you every good wish that may be.
On your birthday and at all other festivals I am
prompt with my congratulatory telegram

– your engagements, weddings, family occasions
call up my willing and anonymous donations,
and although my discreet habit has been to rejoice
for you privately, sometimes my public voice

has defended your honour, one of the dividends
Virtue can count on from having loyal friends.
So when Scandal drags your good name through his filthy
        lists
I am the first to correct gossip columnists

with irate phonecalls and strongly worded letters;
respect is the proper stance towards one's betters.
I speak always for your reputation, with regard
for your honour only, not seeking my own reward.

But recently my own finances have hit a bad patch;

I haven't a single 50 pence piece left to scratch
the back of my chequebook with, let alone piles
of notes to pay gas or electricity bills.

Every day the post brings demands for my overdue
payments, final reminders, licences to renew,
and my bank manager is a usurious tyrant
wanting his pound of flesh with every bank statement

who to ensure a large overdraft enlarges
oppresses me with account and service charges.
It's not that I am extravagant, though I overspend
– I work hard, live a moderate life, make and mend

with an old car, a few hens, a black and white TV
set, as thrifty and economical as you can be.
I do not go in for exotic holidays
in the Fortunate Isles, Manchuria, or the Canaries

but after careful scrutiny might decide
on a week in a rented caravan at the seaside.
The fact of the matter is that I have few vices
apart from the firm habit of ignoring invoices;

I enjoy a monastic diet of bean soup and celery
– salt is the main constituent of my salary.
I never do anything and rarely go anywhere;
what else is there to do, living on fresh air?

It is to yourself then, Lady Moneybags, that I turn,
in the hope that forty years faithful service will earn
recognition at last, and if not wealth untold,
at least some small supplement for my billfold.

I have sacrificed lustful daydreams, grotesque fantasies
of handstitched lapels, silk shirts and a white Mercedes,
lace tablecloths all set about with lapis lazuli

candlesticks, and at every meal fine Chablis

in a Victorian wine glass with a hollow stem
– let those that truly appreciate such things have them.
I renounce all corrupt and bizarre thoughts of sex
on a sprung mattress padded with cashed cheques,

the ecstatic surrender of counterfoils and gilt
edged securities under a luxury quilt
of exchequer bonds, matured policies and the rest
not wishing to overheat a humble nest.

For nothing exotic matches what is said
plainly between loving friends in a firm, hard bed,
while supine comfort yawns and generates
languid ennui where true love suffocates.

A modest request, then, for some of your favours;
freshen me up, resuscitate me with a few fivers,
a Girocheque maybe, containing a tax rebate,
a small brass handshake embossed with today's date,

a lottery ticket with three matching devices
or the pools win that always remedies a crisis,
a sudden windfall from a passing lorry,
any sound credit note issued *To John Gohorry*

a premium bond, a change of heart in banks,
for any one of these, my heartfelt thanks.

Desmond Graham

MRS. THATCHER'S ENGLAND

As the Pole said 'I am learning something
of England here' we saw through the window
a white clad Kung Fu dancer high kick
someone in the face. Next morning
everything was quiet, it being Sunday.
Two lads hauled a cart along what looked like
cobbles from the soft jolts of their load,
the boys being in livery and with that pinched look
the Pole had seen before in Cruikshank.
As their cart paused at the intersection
we saw it was piled high with the bodies
of dead pheasants. For ourselves, we had the choice
of sirloin, saddle of lamb, or pork,
us being four or five and it being Sunday,
and a man in a tall white hat kept sharpening the knife
for us, and listening. We were talking about the North
of England, me having been there and my interlocutors
not, and they were most curious to learn.
On the walls were portraits such as I had seen
in galleries and enquiring of the exploits
of those famous men I learnt they were the ones
who had paid handsomely for the upkeep of this place;
and I was shown a book comprising its history
from before the First World War, how soandso
had signed and witnessed, wagered on the numbers
of the fallen, and the duration of a battle, for a case
of claret or a magnum of champagne. That evening,
thinking to have heard a fox amongst the dustbins
we ventured down and saw an old man rummaging,
but he left and would not be persuaded to return.
A younger man of equally distressed appearance
was crouching by the heater in our stairwell
but he was gone before our visitors went home.

They had come on bicycles, and only in the morning did we learn that as he straightened up from bending to undo the lock, his wife beside him, a passing stranger struck him with full force in the face.
'No use phoning the police,' explained the gate keeper, 'they take half an hour. Are you from here yourself?'

Paul Groves

THE DIVINE CONTENDER

Can you remember when we lay awake all night,
wondering if we'd made the right decision?
Or we wept. Or we dreamt of swords
and retribution, avenging angels singling us out
for fiery displeasure. Yet we had been
conscientious, each of us reading
ten thousand poems, carefully, seeking –
even in the deplorable – some saving feature.

Our short lists were nuggets panned from
the flashing streams of innumerable consciousnesses;
we hoarded them jealously. They were
a heavenly host, a roll call of the redeemed.
But we were looking for more. We were looking
for God: the perfect poem, the entry which would merit
one million pounds, the donation of an anonymous
        benefactor
– some rambling billionaire under his own

strict regime of house arrest, a prisoner
of luxury, fearful of daylight. And we, the judges,
were many in number, reading for eight hours a day
for months on end – under, in fact, a different sort
of house arrest, one much less glamorous.
When, finally, we reached our tortuous decision
the divine contender mysteriously emerged,
a magnificent stranger stepping out of the multitude,

strong and handsome, with immaculate features.
It commanded more than our attention. It demanded
praise, obedience, worship. We fell down
below its thirty short lines, dazzled
and dumbstruck, marvelling that our shared language

could produce such compelling elegance,
such an over-whelming, commanding presence.
The identity of its author was soon revealed:
a prince among men, a person gifted
beyond comprehension. For the prizegiving
he was accompanied by two male warders.
Brought from Broadmoor in a Black Maria,
he strolled, bright-eyed, into the limelight.
Cameras and microphones. Crowds and flowers.
Champagne. A marquee. His laughter was contagious:
a rare sickness; a new, strange music.

David H.W. Grubb

Two Weeks after my Father's Death we Pick the Pears

Two weeks after my father's death we pick the pears from
     five trees.
My mother wanted to leave them but here I am swinging
     in this tree.
The pears are ready. We have timed it just right.
Old bark bruises my back; green dust gets into my sweat.
I work until the moon starts its first rattle across the sea.

Each pear is handed down and inspected by mother.
Kneeling on the steps she places each fruit in a box.
Every pear has to be looked at carefully. There is order
here and some craft.

This is no time to be afraid. In the coming months
I can see her treating letters, papers, words, memory
in the same way.

John Gurney

AT THE PALMIST'S

I falter at the toll-house of the pier.
The price is cheap, and yet I hesitate
as if I cross a threshold, felt the fear
of breaking a taboo. I push the gate,
then step along the left side of the deck.
The Roxy Disco's empty, and the bars
are stagnant, full of shadows. Like a wreck,
the pier-head lists, is tilting. Angular,
I watch the way the off-shore wind behaves.
It leaves its sets of palm-prints on the waves.

She who reads the wisdom of the skin –
Veronica is waiting at the end.
She shivers in her kiosk. Long and thin,
her hands are strongly psychic and extend
some way into the ether. All her panes
are shaded with a notice – articles
on positive disorder that explain
the chaos that is holy, miracles
from random acts of beauty – though her fee
is not part of the glorious anarchy.

I view the door. Its handle's tarnished brass
is darkened by the sea-wind and the brine.
Fingerprints appear, of every class.
I scan the different patterns' changing lines
that tangle, intermingle: scrutinise
skin-carvings of an arch, a whorl, a loop
that speak the inner nature: recognise
the fumbler and the lover and the dupe,
a hand that pulled the door, then with a sigh
prepared to hear the date it had to die.

I stop again, as if I sensed a threat.
Perhaps she is a traveller, far away
in India, or the mountains of Tibet,
engaged with some Supernal. I delay.
One rap upon the door will fetch her back
to sink into some transcendental prayer
then tremble at my palm-prints, scan their tracks
of splintering psychosis, reading there
the artist's map of suffering. Cold and numb
I rap the glass. My fingers hide my thumb.

Sophie Hannah

WRONG AGAIN

I did the right thing once (may God reward me);
Restrained myself. I took a moral stance.
Virtue, I found, was not my thing – it bored me
Rigid, and I would like another chance
To earn myself a wicked reputation
Equal to yours. I'll match you sin for sin.
Lies, promiscuity, inebriation –
It all sounds lovely. When can we begin?
I used to be afraid of rumours spreading.
You made my fear seem fussy, immature.
Here's my new motto, then: just change the bedding
And carry on exactly as before.
A single, happy night beneath your quilt
Is all I want. I'll risk post-coital guilt.

Mike Harding

DADDY EDGAR'S POOLS

Each week you, Thursday Millionaire, would conjure up
The ju-ju, stab the coupon with a pin
Or read the cups, perm my age and height
With Hitler's birthday and the number of
The bus that passed the window and the clump
Of pigeons on the next door neighbour's loft.

With rabbit's foot, white heather, and wishbone
You fluenced the coupon that I ran to post.

Each muggy Saturday you sat still while the set
Called out into the hushed room where I sat
With burning ears and heard a London voice
Call names as strange as shipping forecasts through the
    air:
Hamilton Academicals, Queen of the South,
Pontefract United, Hearts of Midlothian,
Wolverhampton Wanderers, Arbroath, Hibernian,
And once, I thought, a boy called *Patrick Thistle.*

Then every week after the final check,
When Friday's dreams were scratched out with a squeaky
    pen,
You took down from upstairs your brass band coat,
Gave me the wad of polish and the button stick.
And there in that still, darkened room I polished up
Each brassy button world that showed my face;
While you on shining tenor horn played out
Your Thursday Millionaire's lament
For a poor man's Saturday gone.

David Harsent

ELIMINATION DANCING

Not that she cared
a fig about
torchlit dramas
under a hail of umlauts,

the ghettos, or news
of worse things happening at sea,
though dreams often gave her
to the men of the Maquis –

morse like boogie
and peppery cheroots.
Cheek by jowl
with partners who smiled like mutes

she swept the floor;
any second-rater
looked good with her.
Not that she cared, but later

with her back to the wall
and the Devil to pay
she got up on her toes
for the boy in the red beret.

David Hartnett

THE FLEECE

We went to the hovel of the midnight shearer
And lay together, naked, on a wooden board.
Swiftly his sharp-toothed comb skimmed and whirred
Peeling back the fleece our love had grown
Until it dropped away, limp in the straw,
Still warm from us, a loosened milky gown,
Though brambles snagged and blood-spots dabbed
    the wool.
I saw him knead its softness to a roll.
Then through wicket gates to a dark field
Weightless, we ran and lay together, numb.
Prickling stars of sweat our skins bristled
Until, wherever limb brushed against limb,
A luminous froth uncurled, shivered into flame.
By dawn what fleece had clothed us, new or old?

Paul Henry

LEAVING TOWN

Hunting for silence again,
has left the dumbfounded equation
twitching on the computer.

The Capri prods its way out of the stone.
He catches a glider's crucifix
in the sun-roof's v.d.u.

Tall, boyish man prospecting,
something sacrificial in his smile.
He imagines his cooking love,

the tangible soul of garlic
rising from a dead pan
in a damp kitchen miles behind,

or sees the knot between her eyes
tighten as the meal grows cold,
or tastes her curses on his tongue.

He takes in the Eucharist of livestock
where only grass is consumed,
breaking the journey between two churches.

Above the village, God the analyst
idly twirls another cross, a mobile
in a child's airy room.

The fractured house, like an old dog,
waits for him to break the spell.
He dithers between two pluses.

In a different kitchen now, having kissed

his mother at the wooden table,
hunched over the picked at silence,

he dials back down the telegraph poles,
presses another love to his mouth,
hears the wishbone snap in her voice.

Selima Hill

THE DEVASTATION OF EASTER ISLAND

I don't know if you've ever
waited for someone to smile at you,
but if you have, you'll know how I'm feeling now:
all the other smiles for all the other people
fall and melt
like snow from another age
forming rivers where beautiful women are walking
down avenues of trees into the sea;
but all I want
is for *you* to smile at *me*.

I don't know if you've ever
wanted someone to stretch out their hand and touch you,
someone who's been sitting beside you all afternoon
like an uninhabited stone
and driving you mad;
or like a ceremonial stone fish-hook
you're desperate, you're praying, to be fished by –
but if you have,
you'll know how I'm feeling now.

You're numb as hair,
as mute as cats,
as soft as lettuces,
as resolute and mysterious
as the cause of the devastation of Easter Island
where nothing remains except heads,
and a few long-legged chickens
that don't mind drinking sea-water.

I don't know if you've ever
done nothing all day but *languish*,
but if you have, you'll know how I'm feeling now.

Geoffrey Holloway

A Sheaf of Flowers

One side's gone. I'm on your good one.
I put a finger in at your dry fist.
It sucks me, a child at the nipple.
I want more. I won't get it.

Left side of the bed, waving
a sheaf of flowers, she's trying
to raise your eyes.
'Daffs from our garden – look!'

And now she's at you with kisses –
such as the tall daughter with her
may have sprung from,
tangled decades gone.

Around, the block's at its business.
A cook cries over onions,
a porter's out for a drag.
Relatives are told to bring clothes in.

Pneumonia. The stroke. Then gangrene.
To stop you dying quicker, they docked your leg.
You moan when they turn you;
you've that much left.

I remember a cat-mauled finch, it lay
in my hand, heart running faster than life.
Then slowly, lids fell to slits,
down like a curtain, like yours on this bed.

You used to fell race with a fox's flair.
Supple young swam from your eager mating.
But the red man in your blood's tired,

limps distant, heavy.

Time for earth now. The last lap:
stillness under a tree root;
and a quieter kin than daffs –
primrose, windflower.

Robert Hull

AXE

You wouldn't have left it out
inviting comparisons,

though gathering dew
overnight

probably suited it
better than yesterday's

ill-timed fit
of being wielded

on jarring heart-wood
and let skid

vertiginously
off missed edges.

Now I can't wrestle it
out of an obstinate

refusal to resume,
it won't (head hunched

in the block's
grip) relinquish

its tenacious
inertia.

From a distance
it has the posture

of The Thinker –
wondering what

it might next be hurled at,
grimly nostalgic

for the better-
aimed sort of life

it once had
with you, father.

Chris Hurford

RAY
(for Florence Ellen Betts)

Shadowy, he stood at the bottom of the bed,
in a cloud of blue tobacco smoke,
obscured by brilliance and bars of sunlight.
His hair slicked back, and ready for a walk.

And he had that look on him,
that surprised, affronted grin,
tilting like a beaten tree
across his long ploughed field of a face.

Apparently I'd promised, last night
I'd promised, and here I was, still dreaming,
missing the early worm, the postman,
an awesome breakfast with him.

But all this was lost on me
as he moved forward into the daylight,
so I turned to dither in another dream
of a lost chiaroscuro by some Old Master.

An alchemist in his study at dawn,
offers a retort and a crucible
to his snoring apprentice. The boy dreams
of dust or nothing after a night's failed vigil,

but the old man motions
to the blackened alembic, saying:
Here's the pestle and here's the sunlight.
It's all you need, now make gold – make it!

Kathleen Jamie

THE PANCHEN LAMA RIDES FROM LHASA TO KUMBUM
(A thousand miles in a single night)

Now the sky is saddled with stars,
a saddle of stars thrown over the hills' back;
night is a horse leaping the mountains,
night is a nomad shifted by morning,
the Panchen Lama rides hard out of Lhasa
low and clung to the horse's mane,
clings to the mane strung like a comet,
and clear of the darkened back-streets chants
to the ready ear, pale as a conch shell
the thousandth tantra's thousandth cycle,
and horse and Lama quit their earthly forms.

That night a wind crossed snow and pasture:
ruffled the feathers of sleeping rivers,
whirled like a cloak round the shoulders of mountains.
The plateau of Tibet
stretched away like an oil-dark painting
to the grass-land, where in tethered yurts
families wrapped in yaks-wool, slept;
and warm-flanked yaks shifted in their dreaming,
and certain dogs
who opened their jaws to the flying hoof-beat
with an invisible gesture of the Lama's hand
were silenced and charmed.

So for a thousand miles:
till the sun coaxed the world to open like a daisy;
splashed gold on the roofs on the gold-rooved monastery,
of the far side of the precious and protecting hill
at will assumed their mortal shape,
and the youngest boy-monk who rushed from the temple,
his face as round as a gong of wonder

to touch the robe, grab the reins, receive a blessing
and though that boy lived to be a hundred
he always swore
the Panchen Lama
winked.

(This is no story, desperate and apocryphal,
the horse is rumoured to be divine.)

As the Lama rode to the golden roofs
so the rays of the sun lead to the golden sun
so the wild stories come together
round a burning campfire
and the pewter path over the grassland
is a straight track.
So we are come. We turn over the stones
of the past as if reasons
and beginnings scuttled beneath,
and the rumours we repeat to ourselves
converge on truth.
The desert spoke in false voices tho' alluring,
but we can close the door softly and be gone,
with what we own
                    we must carry and bear.
And our horse mayn't be divine,
we must ride it and be astonished and glad
to arrive at a clutter of gold roofs
cupped in a valley:
with a scented tree
whose every leaf
shimmers with the face of the divine.

Lucien Jenkins

The Enclosure Acts

Ta was common so we didn't say it.
My family belonged to too many classes
to risk relegation. Sod was common.
My father only said that when he dropped
a cigarette. Pop music was common
so we didn't listen to it. We weren't common.

My father called trunks 'bathers'. That was common.
At dinner he'd stand in front of the fire
between courses. That was very common.

Meanwhile we each owned our uncommon land,
fenced it in and worked it alone. We held
nothing in common and we had nothing
in common, digging behind tall hedges.

Mike Jenkins

from GRAFFITI NARRATIVES

"UP TO £50,000 GO FISH!"

Took it to-a fishmongers
jus' t' get it weighed
"Aye there's a rainbow, son,
but wha' 'appened to-a trout?"
Took it to-a laboratrees
t' see if it wuz rare
an' they tried t' slice it open
but the colours all went dirty.
Took it to-a surgree
t' try an' get it 'ealed
but the doctor says, "You're crazy!"
when I tol' 'im it wuz truth revealed.

Took it to-a cemetree
placed it by 'er stone,
waited f' 'er voice t' free
watched the evenin' sun
bring them colours back agen,
'eard 'er whisperin' to me
"One day they'll be payin'
50,000 pound f' fish, my lovely
an' wha' yew got there
int worth nothin 'ardly:
'cept it's risen me up
an' give me summin'.
Now take it back, love,
to where it d' belong."

Afta, it swum straight inta
the air by the river,
I'm shewer I 'eard dogs 'n' kids

in the echo o' green an' silver:
it formed a bridge once agen
though I couldn' walk over,
so I went with darkness, my on'y friend
t' make ower 'eadlines,
t' make 'em wheel-fiends wonder:
my dead mam's words prophesin',
takin' minds away from destinations
makin' 'em troubled fer explanations.

Sylvia Kantaris

ANIMALS

Something fishy going on next-door-but-one,
and she's no chicken. Mutton dressed as lamb,
the missus says. Must be cuckoo if she thinks
we can't see through the privet. Some young stud
(can't be more than thirty) strutting up the path
like a tom as if he owned her old man's place,
though she keeps it like a pigsty, that's a fact.
You should hear some of the noises they make.
Once, the wife heard her yelping, thought she might
need help, but we didn't interfere, just in case...
well, what with what you read in the papers –
and I can tell you both our doors are double-bolted –
he could have had a twelve-bore up his jeans,
on top of which we think she might be dangerous
(been to Green-and-Common, my old woman says).
I bet the bugger's sizing up what he can pinch.
That property must be worth a bit. The bitch
is begging for it when you come to think.
Bloody Welfare State keeps *him* in rut,
milking the taxpayers. It gets my goat,
working like a donkey to support subversives,
at it every day like fucking rabbits. ('Scuse my French!)
The cow even protested against Neighbourhood Watch.

Oh love! As if the world were watching us!
As if each of our meetings were a TV summit!
What am I scared of? Hold me closer, tight.

David Kelly

RAW MEAT

Fresh from the abattoir, rough Dougie booted
Suddenly at our back door, arms full of blood
And what could have been the carcass of a cow
Flayed raw. His barrelled arms, more used to brawling
Offered up his clumsy gift. "I browt you this.
Thowt you might like a bit to give to't kids."

"Oh, Dougie, no." More reflex than rejection.
Still your gentle put off was enough, he felt
The snub. Never slow to take the huff he humped
Its weight, shouldered up the hunk of reeking meat. Blood
Squeezed out, spattered the flagstones at his hob-nailed
    feet.
The damage done, you could have bitten out your tongue.

A moment's chevelled awkwardness and that was that.
Dougie wouldn't hear apologies or efforts
To backtrack. "Nay missus then I'll gi' it dogs.
Dogs need feeding just the same as kids. I only thowt…"
Almost embarrassed to, he spat it out. "Your John,
He's only one to crack wi' me and gi' me cigs.

He's alreet John." Praise of your husband damned you
    even
Further into being wrong. You just wanted him gone
But it bothered you, the sullenness of his retreat;
You're bothered still. And this raked up tale you tell
    (because
He barely nods acknowledgement across the street)
Has Dougie at our door again – armed with raw meat.

James Kirkup

HOMAGE TO RIMBAUD
(The Sonnet of the Vowels)

A – crimson, August, pavilion of blood,
summer fanfares, fading into eloquence
of E – a bitter orange solitude
in castled autumn's golden decadence
midwinters invalid I – pale lemon.
Then green exclamatory O of spring –
emerald garlands of snow and blossom!

Ultramarine and azure seasons bring
blue U back into June – deep sapphire mists
ghosting the sleepless lamplight's rosy panes
to deepen dawn's faint lilac-tinted rains
in liquid violet of sombre Y –
symbol of symmetry and ancient trysts,
midnight groves, mystic indigo July.

Helen Kitson

Another Night In The Vice Squad

Just another night: any old night,
working for the Vice Squad. The youngsters
blush red but nothing bothers me;
I just look nonchalant while a prostitute
pours me a coffee, & one for herself.

But that's not a girl, that's a man:
the ones with perfect hair & nails
are the men. The girls are just sluts
who sit in front-room windows eating ice-creams.
They send their daughters to fancy schools,

they send their sons back to the fathers.
It's not that I disapprove: I'm not scared
of AIDS, I let them bring me drinks,
we share cigarettes, we talk about men.
Most of them are really friendly:

I wouldn't say we were bosom-buddies
but it's nice to have a woman to talk to
about girls-things, infections & clothes.
Kerb-crawling's a crime, but men get away with it;
we know it's the women who take the blame.

Last night was good, a punter threw up
when we told him he'd been done by a man,
a tranny biding her time till the op
(they have to live as women, they have to find
the money from somewhere). It was a giggle.

The whore just smiled & checked her nails.
Did you know you look like Cher?
She nodded, then she swore at her punter.

You have admire someone choosing to be
a woman, a victim. And she just smiled.

Stephen Knight

THE BODY-PARTS LAUNDERETTE
(for Sacha Brooks)

Four legs go in: the headboard's next: it's grey,
it's cold where a birdcage and a bed in sections
furnish the space outside The Last Chance antique shop.
At sundown, in the launderette, every day
long, neon striplights twitch into life –
light spills across the pavement like a knife.
Windows mist. Shapes move inside and the evenings drag.
The sounds of agitation never stop.
Stuffed with handbills or copies of the local rag,
the letterbox is down at ankle-height.
Footprints lead away in all directions.
The Body-Parts Launderette is open through the night.

In the window, cards and leaflets face the street
like ghosts: the Car Boot Sale that came and went;
    masseurs
without surnames; *RADIOS FOR SALE*; School Fêtes.
When the ancient machinery shivers and purrs,
puddles appear from cracks in the concrete floor
then seep towards strategically-placed, steel grates.
There's a pay-phone; a bin; a woman's calf
and the patron saint of The Body-Parts Launderette,
Dennis Nilsen, watching from a photograph
nailed to the Supervisor's padlocked, metal door.
One laundry basket's filled with odd feet
customers have left behind. It's dripping wet.

The Supervisor, for her sins, wears
fluffy mules and a quilted dressing-gown.
She burnishes the hacksaws, chains and knives
hung from the yellowing walls; or gathers up
the ticked and folded questionnaires

that quiz the customers about their empty lives.
Have you used **1)** *An acid bought in town*
2) *Soap, or* **3)** *Detergent in a paper cup?*
Somewhere between a coma and a dream,
alone, on plastic seats, they pass whole days
in front of tedious machines; watching the steam,
the suds, those churning reds and greys.

Aileen La Tourette

GIFT HORSES

The summer you don't go away to the water,
You don't tear off your clothes and wear a sort of halter
    and saddle
Over your aureoles, nipples and pubes,

That summer you see what happens at home in the heat,
Like staying up all night to see what the dark does
To the tables and chairs, and getting badly scared,

You meet the same floppy body in your everyday life
Without the tactful waves to cover it up,
Without the sand to make it disappear,

Only your old summer clothes which hide nothing,
Your fake jewels and your old face in the same glass
Burnished with summer like shimmering water,

Things swim towards you out of that shimmering,
Out of the pool of all the houses and the melted people,
Things swim towards you like little sea-horses

Spinning up and down like yo-yos or carousel horses,
But they come in like burglars because you're there,
Mirror-images of burglars who ring up to find you in,

And give you things you don't want but you take
Like the salt in salt water, because you can't not,
You can't even jump the waves and scream and hold
    someone's hand,

Because everyone's holding yours, and the waves come in
    low,
Sea-horses coiling and uncoiling, holding your eye,

You remember reading somewhere how delicate they are,

And now you hold your breath and almost hope
They won't make it but not quite,
Which is all it would take to make them go away,

Instead you watch them wafting like Pegasus,
White as foam, every piece of every other summer
Galloping into your ears and eyes and nostrils

Like grateful horses making for the stable
While you stand there with your mouth open,
Showing off long yellow teeth like a case of trophies.

Gwyneth Lewis

PENTECOST

The Lord wants me to go to Florida.
I shall cross the border with the mercury thieves,
as foretold in the faxes and prophecies,
and the checkpoint angel of Estonia
will have alerted the uniformed birds
to act unnatural and distract the guards

so I pass unhindered. My glossolalia
shall be my passport – I shall taste the tang
of travel on the atlas of my tongue –
salt Poland, sour Denmark and sweet Vienna
and all men in the Spirit shall understand
that, in His wisdom, the Lord has sent

a slip of a girl to save great Florida.
I shall sear through Europe like a standing flame,
not pausing for long, except to rename
the occasional city; in Sofia
thousands converted and hundreds slain
in the Holy Spirit along the Seine.

My life is your chronicle; o Florida
revived, look forward to your past,
and prepare your perpetual Pentecost
of golf course and freeway, shopping mall and car
so the fires that are burning in the orange groves
turn light into sweetness and the huddled graves

are the hives of the future – an America
spelt plainly, translated in the Everglades
where palm fruit hang like hand grenades
ready to rip whole treatises of air.
Then the S in the tail of the crocodile

will make perfect sense to the bibliophile

who will study this land, his second Torah.
All this was revealed: now I wait for the Lord
to move heaven and earth to send me abroad
and fulfill His bold promise to Florida.
As I stay put, He shifts His continent:
Atlantic closes, the sheet of time is rent.

Herbert Lomas

EGG ON A MANTELPIECE

Some parchment-skinned Chinese
painted these boats, this pagoda,
this high peak and these
incomprehensible characters
for a pittance
on this eggshell.

In bad taste as well.
So thin a duster could break it,
and given in love,
it's lasted for years.

All history resides
on a souvenir
from a hen's insides.

Roddy Lumsden

Twenty Haiku for My Dentist

The waiting room is empty.
The fish come up for air.
You beckon me.

Clouds through frosted glass.
Your partners, indifferent,
walk through in white coats.

Around me, you place the bib.
I am not demeaned.
Beneath, we're human.

You leave the room to take
a picture of me. Please,
take me in profile.

The taste of metal
on my tongue. I learn
the physics of attraction.

My hand clutches
my arm a little tighter.
You talk above the whirr.

These words somehow slow
the drill as you repeat them,
somewhere above me.

The grinding drill you call
my favourite part. How did
you know? 'A rough guess.'

You are older than you look.

It doesn't bother me,
and then it does.

The outside world
has become the task. You fix
the clamp inside my mouth.

Anaesthetic. My present
self is a swirling one.
I smell your hair.

Camille Claudel,
you'd maim me, were I Rodin,
and make me think again.

Cautiously, I eye
the nurse. She makes amalgam.
No jealous sparkle.

One fact cannot escape me.
That warmth at my temple
must be your breast.

The radio holds
the room's stasis. Sweet lyrics –
Your instruments' names.

You ask me to take
a heavy bite. Peep inside
my cheek now, voyeur.

Your gloved fingers track
my lips, but never trace. Now,
come outside with me.

Your name on the plaque
outside. The pub across the street

has just opened.

With moist hands, I hold
my numb face. Winter sunlight
is claiming the street.

Reluctantly, I submit
your small signature
on the prescription.

Glyn Maxwell

STARGAZING

The night is fine and dry. It falls and spreads
the cold sky with a million opposites
that, for a spell, seem like a million souls
and soon, none, and then, for what seems a long time,
one. Then of course it spins. What is better to do
than string out over the infinite dead spaces
the ancient beasts and spearmen of the human
mind, and if not the real ones, new ones?

But, try making them clear to one you love,
(whoever is standing by you is one you love
when pinioned by the stars): you will find it quite
impossible, but like her more for thinking
she sees that constellation.
After the wave of pain, you will turn to her
and, in an instant, change the universe
to a sky you were glad you came outside to see.

This is the act of all the descended gods
of every age and creed: to weary of all
that never ends, to take a human hand
and go back into the house.

Roger McGough

Squaring Up

When I was thirteen and crimping my first quiff
Dad bought me a pair of boxing-gloves
In the hope that I would aspire to the Noble Art.

But I knew my limitations from the start:
Myopia, cowardice and the will to come second.
But I feigned enthusiasm for his sake.

Straight after tea, every night for a week
We would go a few rounds in the yard.
Sleeves rolled-up, collarless and gloveless

He would bob and weave and leave me helpless.
Uppercuts would tap me on the chin
Left hooks muss my hair, haymakers tickle my ear.

Without gloves, only one thing was clear:
The fact that I was hopeless. He had a son
Who couldn't square up. So we came to blows.

Losing patience, he caught me on the nose.
I bled obligingly. A sop. A sacrifice.
Mum threw in the towel and I quit the ring.

But when the bell goes each birthday I still feel the sting
Not of pain, but of regret. You said sorry
And you were. I didn't. And I wasn't.

Jamie McKendrick

HOME THOUGHTS

The airmail from India, a weatherbeaten blue,
with wax marks from the candle you had used
to write by reached me. You write that reach
is what travellers there do rather than arrive
being more respectful to the gods of place.
For years your letters from around the world
have kept on reaching me wherever
I'm hunched beside an atlas and a lamp.
When you last saw me I was living in a room
across the road from but a floor below
the room we used to share ten years ago.
Only kindness stopped you saying
it took me quite some time to cross that road;
and looking from my window I expect to see
myself looking out to where in ten years time
I'll be looking back again to see… the last things
you mention are the Parsee towers of silence
where the dead are left for vultures to attend.
I warm to that. It sort of brings things home.

Christine McNeill

SECOND LANGUAGE

'De-furrer,' you explained to your German guest,
who, before refilling the kettle, examined its inside
carefully. He held the little iron plate
between his fingers. 'De-furrer,' you said again.
'De-fürer,' he repeated. You nearly died
for it was just what you'd asked your family
not to mention: der Krieg, der Führer.

His hands were pale, and loving almost,
as he tried to grasp this concept
of descaling. 'You leave it
in the kettle all the while?'
'Yes,' you said, and shook with suppressed
laughter – that English sense of laughing
at the world when really laughing at oneself.

You shook and shook, and he just stood,
quietly observing you, shifting the metal
plate between his fingers,
then pressing it into his palm.
He closed his palm. And still you laughed,
taking refuge in a corner of your kitchen.
Your laughter was a white horse

riding between your shoulderblades.
He raised his closed right hand.
'Your shoelace is undone,' he said.
Immediately you bowed, bent down,
and, fastening the lace, looked up at him.
There was a crumb in the corner of his mouth.
But you were afraid to point it out.

Angela McSeveney

Kirsty

The radio reports the disappearance
of a seven year-old wearing a blue
quilted jacket and brown lacing shoes.

My stomach clenches
as it did thirteen years before
on an empty building site.

The cement bag spread beneath me
stuck to my back.

Christopher Middleton

LAMPOON

1
The man across the street I thought was mad
Is playing catch this evening with a lad.

I hear the ball he flings plop into the glove
Worn by the lad, who's husky. Is it love?

Can love have cured him for a time? Or God?
The man has dialectically changed. How odd.

2
Push it aside, the surface image. Shove
The husky lad away, the baseball glove –

Recall another scene: J. Edgar Hoover
Drooled over snapshots of his husky lover

Curled up in shorts beside a swimming pool:
O toad-cold passion of 'The Heat' – how cool!

3
My madman, in the winter, scarlet cap
Pulled down around his eyes, I saw him tap-

Dance in the street and scatter in the snow
His brownbag lunch along the wall below

For hungry birds. Once he told me, too,
He used to live right here, where I now do.

4
Then off he crawled. The scarlet cap has gone,
Now shirt tail flaps, his left foot settles on

The broken ground, he lets the baseball fly,
Slow, to be sure, but straight enough. While I

Have scandalous doubts – the lad, is he his son?
Kinsman, or neighbour? Is he his illusion? –

The fact remains that in the USA
It's hard to know, harder still to say.

5
My madman plays the heretic, for once,
If blind Greed is the God of North Americans.

The corpse of instinct spits, when pressed by sport,
A lethal wad into the face of thought:

Yet, healed by sport, not love, that heretic
Can't quench the appetites that make him sick –

Captive of the Social Lie, him too. Down goes
His foot and up the dubious ball he throws.

6
So civilization plays to thwart all dreams:
The depth of life won't surface here, it seems.

He's mad as Hoover still, huffpuffing a sane
Picture of himself, while, yet again

The ball or switch is flicked, the rockets go:
There'll be no scandal. Not a soul will know.

Stuart Milson

Billy and The Pigs

Before we pulled back the fence
they stood in the pen
shifting their bulks grunting,
moving their heads quickly
as if each time was a new idea.

Our dog went and kissed them, unthinking,
with the bond of animals;
as if instinct told him
that the discs of their snouts
poked through the netting for the last time.

Two boars for slaughter, streaked with pink,
as if they had stayed up late and cried.

A bucket lured them to the trailer
and they went without trouble,
leaving a sparrow on the wire
rejoicing in its white breast.

Martin Mooney

GLASS

Annie works in a pub. Sinéad sells rubberwear
and used pornography in a tiny shop
it costs an hour's wages to enter. Joe Cancer,
the Reptiles' drummer, is unemployed.
He follows his nose to Camden Town
and bums the price of a Special Brew.
His fellow travellers work the streets
like salesmen, intimidating and polite.
Grub wakes up and hits the streets as well,
cruises Victoria (worse than useless),
rides the Circle Line for hand-outs
('Spare us some change, mate...'),
then comes up from the underworld again
feeling dizzy, seasick, fragile...
Like a job-hunter, he rehearses
his curriculum vitae: an A level in art,
summer in Europe, winter at home,
then a wet spring on a building site
sweeping floors and sleeping rough.
The first band formed at sixteen, the first
chords came almost a year later
for the school hops and youth club discos
that came to nothing. The guitar
was sold to an off-duty Brit in Stranraer
for a fortnight's beer and roll-ups.
Dole from May to July, hiding in the Tate,
meeting Sinéad under the *Large Glass*,
unleashing one another on themselves
beneath that flawed copy. She found the squat
and on their first night in its attic
tattooed him with red ink and a pin,
a tiny rose and cross... He's near the river
when this train of thought pulls up.

Next stop Shanty Town. Somewhere between
RPG Avenue and the Sydenham bypass
Belfast coughed them up and spat them out –
himself, Annie, Joe, Sinéad, crossing
in ones and twos in their thousands,
life stories taking a turn for the worse.

Paul Muldoon

from Shining Brow

QUARTET

When all's said and done we'd like to know
if Amundsen has reached the Pole.
Has he been struck some cruel blow?
Is he eaten by a whale?
Has he stumbled through a hole?
Is he lying at the bottom of the sea?
Going down,
going down,
going down in history.

At the end of the day we'd like to hear
some word of the anarchist plot
to kill the Emperor
of Japan. How goes it with the suffragettes?
Why was Canalejas shot?
Is China still our cup of tea?
Going down,
going down,
going down in history.

Nineteen twelve. The Greeks and Turks
fight a familiar duel.
The Piltdown Men of Planter stock
scuttle Irish Home Rule.
The *Titanic* founders on a berg.
The passengers cry wee-wee-wee.
Going down,
going down,
going down in history.

Nineteen thirteen. By now Niels Bohr
has cracked the atom's nut.

The Mexican Prime Minister
and the King of Greece are shot.
New leaders roll off the conveyor
belt like Henry Ford's first Model 'T's;
going down,
going down,
going down in history.

Nineteen fourteen. The latest news
has Woodrow Wilson's
warships pounding Veracruz.
All going down. All going down.

Though it's been five years since he fell off a mule
at the San Carlos agency,
Geronimo's still going down,
going down,
going down in history.

June twenty-eighth. As the guests arrive
for a soirée at Taliesin,
a shot rings out in Sarajevo.

Felicity Napier

JASMINE

The hottest July on record – as hot as Spain.
Number fifty-four is a settlement of grief,
shuttered and blind to the street outside.
To a background of the Albinoni that he loved
the telephone rings and rings again, and sounds
of sobbing ebb and flow in the cool dim rooms.
Jasmine twists around the door, scattering
the step with small white stars. A serpent
hose lies curled asleep on the cracked earth.

Beyond the fence another house is in distress;
its back has been removed. Workmen's radios drone
across the lawn where empty deckchairs listen.
Somewhere a piano is being tuned. Inside,
the dog sprawls, refusing to move; goldfish gobble
for oxygen and the lovebird's cage is silted up.
And visitors visit... some wanted, some not.
She drifts through the rooms, in his new blue shirt
with the chain he gave her glinting at her throat.

Meals around the table they brought back from France
last year are rituals that hold the days together.
Friends bring pizza, pasta, coke for the children
and the first small seedless grapes. In the hall
the stacks of unread papers mount; cards and letters
layer the table. And flowers keep coming – drooping
garden roses, glossy pot plants, stiff bouquets.
She has pinned his smiling photograph everywhere –
that lean face, now an icon, continues to shock.

The crisis dwindles. Her friends start to fall away;
the children return to school; the airless nights pass
and yet, like the sickly sweetness of the jasmine,

his absence won't go away. It shadows her all day.
But soon she will learn the art of self-defence:
she won't buy more coffee beans or make his lentil soup;
she won't run down a street, pursuing his look-alike.
And, in the dark, sleepless hours, when that clear voice
calls out to her, she will train her heart not to leap.

Dennis O'Driscoll

MISUNDERSTANDING AND MUZAK

You are in the Super Valu supermarket
expecting to meet me at 6.15.

I am in the Extra Valu supermarket
expecting to meet you at 6.15.

Danny Boy is calling you down special-offer aisles.
Johann Strauss is waltzing me down special-offer aisles.

I weigh mushrooms and broccoli and beans.
You weigh beans and mushrooms and broccoli.

It is 6.45. No sign of you.
It is 6.45. No sign of me.

You may have had a puncture.
I may have been held up at work.

It is 6.55. You may have been murdered.
It is 6.55. I may have been flattened by a truck.

Danny Boy starts crooning all over you again.
Johann Strauss starts dancing all over me again.

Everything that's needed for our Sunday lunch
is heaped up in my trolley, your trolley.

We hope to meet somewhere, to eat it.

Stuart Paterson

SECOND SKIN

Your clicking fingers gathered a frail rope
From the hills, conjuring warmth back into
Wool, weaving unspoken worries through
The frame of my chest, let my thin shoulders
Harness a tapestry patterned with you.

A decade hangs between the man and boy
You strove to warm. I worry that I'll miss
Cold sometimes. The cuffs have begun to frizz,
Wisps occasionally sloughing to the floor.
I carry you as you carried me before,
Or slip into remnants of old lovers
Made by others whose hands were not so sure.

Now I walk the hills in winter sun
That sends no heat and wrap myself around
Old sitting-stones; let the softened armour
Shield my skin and stroke my neck, a blanket
Holding a language of hands together,
Straightening my back by the precipice
Of dark-water light. The lambs on the crest
Must yield their coats. Not me. I breathe the twine
Of ribbed bone. One bloody thorn and I fall
Untangled and cold to a grave of air.

Christopher Pilling

TIME FOR CHANGE

The clock face hardly changes;
its hands are not meant to touch –
they swivel from a centre, their ranges
only so far, never too much.

Minutes step with an even gait,
clockwork even, always just
catching up. There's a spate
of ticks to tell before the rust.

They set the pace and we must follow
suit. Their tricks are crotchets
that voice each catch. Swallow
your axis and try out duets.

Stephen Plaice

Last Café in the West

In that town you've always passed through
thinking 'What a place to wind up in' –
one day you'll have to stop and try the café,
if only to put its melancholy to the test.

The steamed-up windows warn it's a trap
where the tea's been stewing all summer
and the special menu's left scrubbed blank.
You break the crust on the sugarbowl –

the jukebox fuzzes a Glitter hit,
there's just the waitress playing the fruit-machine
even though she knows it's fixed –
she'll talk to you because you smell of the city.

She wants to get away from here and act,
to leave the local champion practising out back,
she doesn't want to be his girl any more
and turn into the woman in the upstairs flat.

You'd take her too if the last chapter of Angels
didn't burst in, snap the chairs to beating bats
and leave the walls bleeding ketchup,
the waitress love-bitten and her tears unpaid.

You won't defend her – she'll wait for the next,
or take a chance on the soldier from the camp,
after too many vodkas at the dinner-dance,
and get pregnant down a lane in the van.

She only stayed here this long to play a cameo
in the dream you've been filming along this road.
Next time you come looking for the location:

clear glass, antiques, the woman in the upstairs flat,

still in a nightdress, her hair in a mess,
shouting down: *it closed up some summers back*,
as the red lens of the sun pans out on you –
last customer of the last café in the West.

Richard Price

HINGES

On the airstrip: fog.
Nothing taking off.
Five in the afternoon,
more or less.

I'd have called it a 'flitting'
but it was a year before I was born –
to my father it was 'moving house.'
He was Ma's envoy in Scotland:
he'd just chosen a field
that would grow into a bungalow
and he'd pay for it
whenever the bathroom,
opening on the hall
with a frosted glass door,
trapped her, towelnaked,
before the postman
and something to be signed for.

Through the same melted glass
I saw my first memory:
my eldest brother, nine or ten,
was stretching and not touching anything,
petrolburns on his face and hands,
a human X at the front door
(on a building site a friend
had clicked him alight;
we still don't know the bet).

On the airstrip: fog, night.
Eleven o'clock. My father is being practical
on the hotel phone: 'I am speaking
back in my room.'

In the morning in England, like a new couple
two police officers stood back
as Ma opened the door.
They had to be reassured:
she gave them tea in the fine bone.
(Just beyond the wicker of radar
the first plane out, just past midnight,
had dropped like a figurine.)

In the afternoon
my mother met my father in Arrivals.
Before they held held held each
other he says they shook hands.

Peter Redgrove

LAMPS AND FIRE

The pale phlegm of the oyster,
Its satin mucus-and-muscle,
A big black pearl inset;

It looks like a putrefact,
But it is phlegm and fortune.
What does it feel, its mantle-lip

Studded with sky-blue eyes –
Like an Aurora, an Ezekiel-angel,
An aware arch of firmament,

An Argus peering out of a river-bottom?
Any true Christian
Views the male human body

As the centre of experience;
While the men debated at table
Over their oysters,

She busied herself behind them
With lamps and fire.

Mark Robinson

DOMESTIC BLISS

The mess gets worse as the beautiful world
tries harder, expands on its original mistake –
something crass blurted out in a fluster –
making a monument out of moleshit.

You and I aren't bothered. Too busy to
beat the wolves from the doorstep, too tired
to be concerned about anything, tonight
the blackcurrant wine is dyeing our tongues

the colour of our hearts. We're saying what we mean,
for once, and it feels good, making plans
for the future as if there were no tomorrow.
Your smile leaps out from behind your teeth.

We can do whatever we want.
What we want to do now is
get sordid in front of the fire.
The world is hard but worth it.

Stephen Romer

Cautionary Tale

In contemplation at the café:
a dazed young man out of Cavafy,

'the poet nearing his twenty-fifth year'
gone from bankrupt to millionaire

in the small white hours of eros.
He walks into a morning of promise

and sunlight, with a world-including smile,
startled to find business as usual,

and on his body the surplus greatcoat
from the hopeless months, with the torn pocket

where coins disappeared in the lining;
the same body too, not hunching along

this morning though, but cock of the walk,
the lover tolerant of discourteous traffic,

exuding the benevolence
of a man whose work has been praised, once,

in the press… Now he's at his zenith
in the café; but the waiter's brisk cloth

is applied to the next door table,
change is ceaseless and imperceptible,

the world is moving round him in his dream,
but the world is moving on without him.

Carol Rumens

Et Incarnatus Est

Windows are often loneliest when lighted,
Their silvery plenitude a kind of treason.
They smile, they seem to offer invitation
Between the last-leafed branches, but their eyes
Are kind only if you possess the keys.
Journeys towards such stars are best diverted.

Desire, though, being the senseless thing it is,
I know a certain window from all angles
And frequencies. The city's whole galère
Contains no poorer version of stained glass,
But it's among the daily miracles
When I check anxiously, find it still there,
Glass being so promiscuous with its spangles,
And light so frail, in cities such as this.

I'm happiest when it's invisible,
Sunk in the fireless black of the night sky,
A lovely emblem folded, put away,
And nothing left more innocent and hopeful
Than life itself. *There's no epiphany,*
No magic room: this is an empty house.
I can unthrone it, if I trust that blackness.

But when, through the burnt-out December trees,
The window shivers dreamily, plays at being
An earth-bound moon, then shows me, bright and full,
That soft shoulder-like curve, that frame of grace,
I breathe like a runner though I'm standing still.
I know what it is to have been a king
Once, and now to be frightened of a stable.

Some windows cut the flesh but this, when lighted,

Is flesh itself, those fluids, sighs, word-world.
Other lights vanish or become blurred.
This burns the wind – not light, but living eyes,
Faultless, candid, where my last hope dies,
A child of hell, its death never completed.

Carole Satyamurti

PASSED ON

Before, this box contained my mother.
For months she'd sent me out for index cards,
scribbled with a squirrel concentration
while I'd nag at her, seeing strength
drain, ink-blue, from her finger-ends
providing for a string of hard winters
I was trying not to understand.

Only after, opening it, I saw
how she'd rendered herself down from flesh
to paper, alphabetical; there for me
in every way she could anticipate
    — Acupuncture: conditions suited to
    — Books to read by age twenty-one
    — Choux pastry: how to make, when to use.

The cards looked after me. I'd shuffle them
to almost hear her speak. Then, the world
was box-shaped (or was I playing safe?)
for every doubt or choice, a card that fitted
    — Exams: the best revision strategy
    — Flowers: cut, how to make them last
    — Greece: the men, what you need to know.

But then they seemed to shrink. I'd turn them over,
find them blank; the edges furred, mute,
whole areas wrong, or missing. Had she known?
The language pointed to what wasn't said.
I'd add notes of my own, strange beside
her urgent dogmatism, loosening grip
    — infinitives never telling love
    lust single issue politics when
    don't hopeless careful trust.

On the beach, I built a hollow cairn,
tipped in the cards. Then I let her go.
The smoke rose thin and clear, slowly blurred.
I've kept the box for diaries, like this.

William Scammell

TRIADS

Three unusual occupations: apologising, not dicing the
carrots, unravelling a woollen hat.

Three fruits fit for a king: the pineapple, the cantaloupe,
the raspberry.

Three properties to beware in a tennis racquet: poor
balance, hairy strings, a shabby grip.

Three accomplishments well-regarded by the middle-
classes: collateral, corner cupboards, a steady backswing.

Three indications of the onset of love: frequent
    showering,
punctuality, a happy concordance of mouth and eyes.

Three excellent times of day: mid-morning coffee taken
at noon, the postman's second call, Frost at Midnight.

Three useful specifics for the hand: a cat's back, a beech's
bole, a woman's arm.

Three habits to be avoided at all cost: saying what you
think, wearing cravats, shopbought firelighters.

Three sorts of story of which there is a superfluity:
adventure stories, funny stories, sad stories.

Three makes of car it would be idle to aspire to: a
Lamborghini, a Rolls Royce Silver Shadow, a De Lorean
    Goosewing.

Three things recommended by famous authors:

the bicycle,
then nightingale, death.

Three methods of entering a crowded room: politely,
dejectedly, Robert Redfordly.

Three not needed on voyage: estate agents, sports
commentators, beauticians.

Three superlative kitchen sights: a wall-mounted tin-
opener, a synod of jugs, a wooden table.

Three reproductions to be ambushed at the front door:
Sunflowers, A Bigger Splash, Venus Rising from the
       Waves.

Three demoiselles known to have strayed beyond
       Avignon:
the actress with good cheekbones, the activist who cannot
       aspirate, the fancy that.

Three topics to ponder whilst awaiting sleep: can
presuppositions be presupposed? the exact topography
aroused by the smell of clean linen? what will it be like
after?

Jo Shapcott

Vegetable Love

I'd like to say the fridge
was clean, but look at the rusty
streaks down the back wall
and the dusty brown pools
underneath the salad crisper.

And this is where I've lived
the past two weeks, since I was pulled
from the vegetable garden.
I'm wild for him: I want to stay crunchy
enough to madden his hard palate and his tongue,
every sensitive part inside his mouth.
But almost hour by hour now, it seems,
I can feel my outer leaves losing resistance,
as oxygen leaks in, water leaks out
and the same tendency creeps further
and further towards my heart.

Down here there's not much action,
just me and another, even limper, lettuce
and half an onion. The door opens so many,
so many times a day, but he never opens
the salad drawer where I'm curled in a corner.

There's an awful lot of meat. Strange cuts:
whole limbs with their grubby hair,
wings and thighs of large birds,
claws and beaks. New juice
gathers pungency as it rolls down
through the smelly strata of the refrigerator,
and drips on to our fading heads.

The thermostat is kept as low as it will go,

and when the weather changes
for the worse, what's nearest
to the bottom of the fridge starts to freeze.
Three times we've had cold snaps,
and I've felt the terrifying pain
as ice crystals formed at my fringes.

Insulation isn't everything in here:
you've got to relax into the cold,
let it in at every pore. It's proper
for food preservation. But I heat up
again at the thought of him,
at the thought of mixing into one juice
with his saliva, of passing down his throat
and being ingested with the rest
into his body cells where I'll learn
by osmosis another lovely version
of curl, then shrivel, then open again to desire.

Penelope Shuttle

The Reader

Such secrets in books,
but they are all about you.
You read, you are the story,
you are the alien, the courtesan,
the murderer, the nun,
the son, the detective, the hero,
the victim.
You are in every primer, trilogy
and romance, you are on each greasy
page of the pornographies.
You read till you're shaking.
You read till your pockets are full of blood.
You read till your eyes are flying with tears,
you read till your thirst for knowledge
is slaked, and you try to come out
from between the pages.
Your eyelids close,
the book falls to the floor,
now you are just a big old sweet-tempered horse
called Annie,
asleep on your huge delicate pitch-dark hooves,
your great serene lips quivering;
the children reach up to stroke you
and the groom pulls coyly at your mane.

Stephen Smith

THE EXECUTION SHED

The execution shed's 20 x 10
of unadorned scrubbed boards was built outside
B Wing; a covered annexe led the way
from the 'queer' cell which time was recessed from.
No warders were allowed to wear a watch,
a humane gesture beaten by the choice
of the word 'shed'. I looked it up; it means
outbuilding set aside from common use,
a place for beasts or implements. Language
so useful as a gloss to monitor
emotion, consecrated these bare feet.
Its primitive hygiene was like a Non-
Conformist Hut, stripped to the minimal
required for their tight ceremony.
I thought about the draughty flitching shed,
cut through by wind in Armagh, where my mother's
Da skimmed the carcasses of pigs with a wet
knife. Memories of that horror were high camp
compared to this. It is almost wicked
to research by words the final history
of this box-room. There are places that syntaxes
can't close, or conversely unlock;
where bodies devolve back before the soul;
when everything is ornamental
but the movements of the gut and a dead smell.

Peter Street

STILLBORN
For Jenny.

I piss on my hands
to ease burning
from blisters and from frost,
steam in a warm few seconds
dies of cold.

I'm tunnelling underneath
the family headstone,
stacking
cubes of oil-black clay
onto the wooden staging as

black beetle funeral cars creep in
between angels standing either side
of cast-iron gates;

I take from Jenny her baby
and slot him under
a list of names
into Dearly Beloved Grandfather's arms.

Matthew Sweeney

AFTER CLOSING TIME

*'Those who don't believe in life after death should be here after
closing time': notice inside an office in Derry's city cemetery.*

The gate will be open, and streetlights
will guide you through the graves,
but you'd better watch your carry-outs
as the dead are barred from pubs.
Watch for the flowers that fly
from grave to grave, creating letters
for the papers and maybe more dead –
and one thing you'll know in the half-light
is that the dead are too many
to fit in the ground, too lively
to lie in a box, so they do
what you'd expect them to, and that's why
they surround you as you swig
from a can. They ruffle your hair,
breathe through unbrushed teeth,
fart even, and one of the pushier
puts his finger in the hole in his head
then invites you to follow. Another
opens his rotting shirt to show you
his two hearts, the old and the new,
and a one-legged ex-pensioner
eyes the bulge of your cigarettes,
and you'd be well advised to drain
one can, then chuck the other
as far as you're able, for the dead
hate those who outlive them,
and you'd be canny to suss this
and run, and hope the gate's not shut.

R.S. Thomas

PLAS-YN-RHIW

By day it is its own
audience. By night
its lights turn
to sores in the mist.

I have eavesdropped it
too long. It has nothing
to teach but that time
is the spirit's privation.

Memories are voracious.
What is left of my
life after, each day,
they have had their meal?

Morning or evening
up and down between
box on the worn
carpet of my patience.

Faces on long stems
remind. Bird voices
recall, charitable but
shrill... the velvet band

round the throat purring
with complacence. The place
itself is a memorial
to the peremptoriness

of emotions I have nothing
to bring to but pressed
flowers. The century

closes. The writing

of the lichen is too slow
for mind to attend
to. The sky modernises
its cipher and the orchard

where time dozed is
a laboratory for experimenting
with life's seed, where chromosomes
are divided, genes crossed

with genes, and God
shuts his eyes for mutations
to come up with a new
colouring for thought's apple.

Martin Turner

TRESPASSES

'You can't tell the truth *all* the time,'
she says, shaken momentarily by an inkling
of all the fissures conjured up by love.
'What is kindly meant, is not kindly said.'

Face glued to the window. Inside, all the reticence
of beachballs, binoculars, teabags: a man's modest
taproot to creation as he seeks to fold himself
in oblivion before his time.

A spy needs few keys – people always talk
about themselves. Lavender, for instance,
'needs moist, rich soil, not too near the sun'
(the lady visits her garden every morning).

Through the embrasure peeps a picket
from the land of colour, of sun a world away.
'A country of cheerless pasta – all chill,'
announces the visitor in a whisper.

A child frequently finds herself off-limits
in this way, looking up people's noses,
remembering mother's plump, shaved leg,
getting the point without all the traces of argument.

A sky of stormy pewter like the sea.
'Not a single normal placenta in Nova Huta.'
Really? So much lies hidden under a rainbow.
Numbers, like skies, go on forever.

So forgive us our trespasses, our daily bread,
as these transgressions are built, birdlike,
into ziggurats of fastidious ornament

which time does not dishevel,

landmarks by which the traveller reaches
into the interior, paying ever less heed
to thoughts of return, to summoning telegrams;
our truths, beloved of explorers.

Steven Waling

From The Country Of Lost Hats

On the day I arrived
they were holding the Festival
of Red Hats, where the populace rejoiced
in their freedom to wear red hats. A man
with a name made entirely of consonants
gave me a hat as I left the airport,
telling me to wear it or the crowds
would tear me to shreds in an instant.
That night I tell you it rained a deluge;
in the morning flotillas of little hats
sailed down the gutters like burning ships.

That year the hotel I stayed in
was the tallest in the capital
and from my window I could see
all the way to the steel foundries
steaming in the sun like battleships.
People were tolerant when I tried
their difficult language, and smiled
constantly as at the punchline of
some joke that hadn't yet been told.
I bought a pamphlet in English that
spoke of a boom in the production
of shoes, though no-one that winter
wore anything but German boots.

It is now nearly a year
since the day called Change
In The Weather, and I've just
returned from villages in the mountains
where peasants in their national costumes
persuaded the soldiers to take off hats
in a national show of politeness.

But the citizens still wear hats:
some blue, some green, some yellow-
and-brown; no-one admits they ever
wore any colour but these.
There are still no shoes but the boots
fit better on the other foot. In cafés,
however, as the weather on the whole
seems to be warmer, some young men
have taken to going out hatless and
dancing in their stockinged feet.

John Powell Ward

SPELLING

Is he still it now? Is Jesus
It now, or has it changed now? Is

Jesus still it now, King of
Jews like and the world now? Is he

King now still like they said, like we
Kids were told, is he king still of

Love now, like when in the bombs and
Later the rationing, is he son of

Man as they said or at least
Many said, or some said? Oh. He's

Not now. That's all over and done
Now, that's it then. Oh, right,

Oh, so it's over now. Oh well, it's
Over and gone now. Too bad then. Oh.

Susan Wicks

HA HA BONK

Love the Big Bad joke for adults,
electric custard, gooseberry in a lift.
Why couldn't he have come up with something better?
Knock, knock, I got tired of asking.
Irish stew in the Name of the Law.

And why did the Burglar saw the legs off his bed?
So we could hear the springs creak more clearly?
I wanted to lie low too. Very low, lying with you.
Lying all the time if I could.
Was it that I had stolen something?

And now it goes Ha ha bonk
all down the passage.
A Man laughing his head off.
If I see it rolling I shall pick it up,
carry its belly-laugh with me on a silver plate.

Clive Wilmer

AMORES

I call this latest book Adversity.
Though it is mine, it is obscure to me.
Some passages of love, though, seem more clear
In a dark context, and I gloss them here.

*

It was not quite the last time. Yet, that day,
Orgasm shook my body with a cry
That echoed through me like a long goodbye.
We parted; then you wept, and turned away.

*

We first met maybe seven years ago
But barely more than chatted before this.
Three afternoons of love, and you must go.
I miss you, scarcely knowing whom I miss.

*

Those brieze-block walls: bare in my memory
The room is – basin, bed, one lamp, one chair.
Yet, entering it, I found you also bare,
And lay down in the lap of luxury.

*

Strange that of all things I recall this fact:
Neither the surge of passion nor the act,
But falling asleep like a child no terrors shake,
Who can, because the woman stays awake.

Despising though desiring you, I let
Our next date pass, deciding to forget.
I'd known you, say, five hours in fewer days;
Twenty years later, how you touched me stays.

*

I see a broken city in your head
(Beautiful lady) ravaged by cross-fire.
But here, against that backdrop, you are led
By civil urgencies of sweet desire.

*

You speak of hope and liberty, new love.
Why must I speak of loyalty and despair?
Freedom is our two bodies as they move
And hopelessness the passion we must share.

*

I thought myself unscathed, so did not yield,
But ran till, looking back from a safe height,
I saw wrenched bodies on a battlefield
That once had seemed a garden of delight.

*

Dear child, dear lady, bless you where you sleep
Alone, who should be sleeping here with me.
My one desire's that your desire should keep
On beating at the gates of reverie.

Chris Woods

BLOOD PRESSURE

His outstretched arm
is bandaged above the elbow
with a black blood pressure cuff.

She wears the stethoscope
like a personal stereo
and listens to the beat of his pulse.

She squeezes the rubber bulb.
The cuff tightens round his arm
like angina round his chest.

Mercury delivers the message,
pumped upwards
through a thin glass vessel.

The cuff slackens.
She hears his pulse come and go
like air inside central heating.

His arm warms back to life,
waits expectantly, palm up.
She hands over some information:

Not that his heart is changing
to rubber, squeezing blood
through narrow vessels.

Nor that his cerebral arteries
could burst into a stroke
and deaden his arm forever.

Only that he can be treated.

She begins to remove his fears
and his black arm band.

Tamar Yoseloff

IN THE CHELSEA PHYSIC GARDEN

To tell the truth, it's the names and not
the plants that get you, you thrill to Latin,
the 'icus' and 'atum', the beauty of endings.
I like the juicy berries of the belladonna,
the shoo-fly with its little maracas, all
the strange and unloved weeds. Growing up,
the lullabies my mother sang were about
lost love and how sad the past could be,
later. No Rock a Bye, Baby, just the facts.

Now, I love her for it, for the names
she gave me, collections of constellations,
varieties of sea shells, the flowers
we'd pick out walking, bring home to dry.
I used to save abandoned baby birds, frogs
from snakes' jaws. It would always end
in tears. Forgive me, there are things I want
to say, but I have no words, just Proper
Names, more Latin, prosaic American slang.

In the fairy tale version, we are planted,
not side by side, as you might expect,
but in separate hemispheres, never to meet.
You the cool fern, adaptable to rainy climates,
and rain or shine, reliable. I'm the problem,
spiky, dangerous, the occasional flower,
poison of course. But exotic. Experts travel
miles to meet me. I dream of leaves, your
soft caress. I guess I'd slash you to bits.

Benjamin Zephaniah

MAN TO MAN

Macho man
Can't cook
Macho man
Can't sew
Macho man
Eats plenty Red Meat,
At home him is King,
From front garden to back garden
From de lift to de balcony
Him a supreme Master,
Controller.

Food mus ready
On time,
Cloth mus ready
On time,
Woman mus ready
On time,
How Macho can yu go?

Cum
Talk to me bout sexuality,
Cum meditate,
Cum Save de Whale,
Dose bulging muscles need Tai Chi
Yu drunken eyes need herb tea,
Cum, Relax.

Macho man
Can't cook, sew or wash him pants,
But Macho Man is in full control.